Seeking God's Will on Same-Sex Relationships The Experience of Cleveland Friends Meeting

Compiled and edited by Marty Grundy

Printed for Cleveland Friends Meeting by CreateSpace.com
2010

No part of this publication may be reproduced, stored in a retrieval system, or transmitted in any form without the prior written permission of the Clerk of Cleveland Friends Meeting.

Our thanks to Anne E. G. Nydam for the cover design, based on her print "Circle of Angels" © 2007.

Copyright 2010 © by Cleveland Friends Meeting.
All rights reserved.

Minute of Support

With joy-filled hearts, Cleveland Friends Meeting offers a minute of support for the project that has resulted in the manuscript: *The Experience of Cleveland Friends Meeting with Seeking God's Will in Same-Sex Relations*. We participated in the process of creating this book as a Meeting. It chronicles our attempt to follow God, serving as an example of one Meeting's experience in following a right decision and through it, the deepening of our spiritual practice. We share this concrete history to elucidate who we are and what we are trying to do. Our hearts are filled with gratitude to Marty Grundy, for her years of meticulous record keeping, faithful work, and diligent compiling of documents that comprise this manuscript.

- approved by Cleveland Friends Meeting
at our Monthly Meeting for Business, 7/18/2010

Acknowledgements

This book reflects the participation of the members and attenders of Cleveland Friends Meeting and of the meetings with which it was affiliated. The experience was corporate. The pain, the struggle, and the discouragement were shared even when proposed solutions were diametrically opposed. Thanks to all those who "stayed at the table" trying to be faithful to what they believed was God's will.

More recently the current members and attenders of Cleveland Friends Meeting have enthusiastically supported publishing this account. Thanks to all who have helped with the project.

Special thanks go to our former member Anne E. G. Nydam for designing the cover. The text would be littered with too many typographical and grammatical errors if it were not for the eagle eyes of proof readers, especially Tim Damon. Any errors that remain are the responsibility of the editor. Thanks in advance to the committee of Laura Lockledge, Joyce Callahan, Connie Green, and Jo Steigerwald for marketing this book.

Preface

Many Friends across the United States and even abroad are aware that Cleveland Friends Meeting struggled with the issue of same-sex relations for some eight years, and we were eventually disowned from Ohio Yearly Meeting (Conservative) for our sense of a "third way" that opened to us. We felt led to understand that we were not to name that two women had a marriage or not a marriage, but to celebrate their loving relationship and family. It seems right to us now, more than fifteen years later, to publish our experience of coming into unity in the hopes that we may be reminded, and others may learn from it, as we all seek greater willingness to listen for Divine Guidance.

Much of the following compilation was assembled in 1997. In order to provide a fuller understanding and context, additional documents as well as a few personal letters have been added. Unfortunately, a few papers have not been found. Since 1997 the issue has arisen several more times in Cleveland Meeting so additional minutes have been added as the story continues.

At a monthly meeting held Ninth Month [September] 27, 2009, Friends approved putting into print the minutes, reports, and other material documenting our experience. A draft was prepared and circulated for two months. Friends met on Fourth Month [April] 2, 2010 to address stylistic and substantive issues in relation to making this material more widely available.

Our hope is that by presenting the multiplicity of documents—minutes from monthly, quarterly, and yearly meetings, reports of committees, and some letters—rather than by providing a narrative, readers may draw their own conclusions. Passions are still aroused, even so many years later, over homosexuality, same-sex marriage, the processes that were used or misused, and the loss of fellowship that resulted.

Traditionally Friends eschewed the use of pagan-name-based nomenclature for months and days of the week. Documents quoted here sometimes use numbered days and months following old Quaker usage, and sometimes use the common names.

Friends were informed that the inclusion of individuals' names in public documents (such as minutes and reports) are permissible under the law. We decided that for other material, we would use the names of individuals who are still involved with Cleveland Meeting, but would use initials for those who are not.

In order to avoid an over-abundance of quotation marks, documents, including minutes, reports, articles from the meeting newsletter (the *Tatler*), and correspondence, are in normal typeface. Explanations, additional narrative, and other connecting material are in italics. Spelling and capitalization have been corrected. Meeting, for example, is only capitalized when used as the name of a specific organization. Unless otherwise stated, any references to monthly meeting or Ministry and Oversight Committee are assumed to refer to Cleveland Meeting.

Generally speaking, in Cleveland Meeting the clerk facilitates the business, while an assistant clerk or recording clerk writes the minutes which are then usually read back in the face of the meeting for approval or amendment as needed. In Ohio Yearly Meeting (Conservative) and its Representative and Quarterly Meetings, the clerk usually performs both services.

Introduction

In the seventeenth century when the Religious Society of Friends (Quakers) began, an institutional structure was developed to facilitate corporate attention to Divine Guidance without the imposition of a hierarchy of human officials. Instead, a system of geographic, concentric, or hierarchical bodies was organized. The local level that may or may not have had smaller constituent groups, met monthly to conduct the business of the faith community. It was called a monthly meeting. In recent years the sessions of the monthly meeting have often been termed meetings for worship with attention to business. A geographical group of monthly meetings, traditionally on a roughly county basis, met four times a year to consider the affairs of this larger group. They were called quarterly meetings. Finally, a much larger group of quarterly meetings gathered once a year to conduct business for the entire group, called, not surprisingly, a yearly meeting. Over the years as it became clear that there were things that needed the attention of the yearly meeting between annual sessions, Representative Meeting was formed, representing the yearly meeting, with members appointed by constituent meetings. (This body sometimes has a different name in other yearly meetings.)

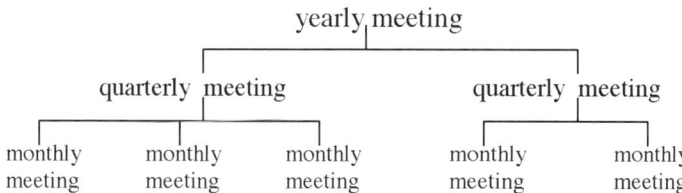

These words—monthly, quarterly, and yearly meetings—mean two things. They are the names for the official bodies and also for the actual sessions when the body meets to conduct business.

Since Friends had no paid priests or pastors the pastoral care, as well as all the other tasks of church governance, had to be performed by members. Friends realized that Divine gifts were bestowed on women and men among them. In time a system of recognizing the holders of these gifts as ministers or elders developed. Ministers and elders found it helpful to meet together for worship and to consider the condition of the meeting as a whole. A system of monthly, quarterly, and yearly meeting committees or "meetings" of ministry and oversight (M&O) arose. In some Friends meetings other names have been substituted such as "ministry and counsel" or "worship and ministry".

Because Cleveland Meeting was incorporated before it became part of a yearly meeting, it has an Annual Meeting, as prescribed by Ohio law. This is usually in May and is combined with a regular monthly meeting. In addition to considering the report of the nominating committee and the next year's budget, there is a State of the Meeting report, usually a similar summary report from Ministry and Oversight Committee, and a message from the clerk.

In the nineteenth century, under the strain of tremendous social, theological, economic, and political changes within the country, the Religious Society of Friends suffered several separations or schisms. Each splinter took some parts of the original charism and ignored others. Each reached out to compatible non-Quaker denominations and over time came increasingly to mirror them, losing still more of the wholeness of the unique Quaker insight. These divisions remain.

At one time there were three Ohio Yearly Meetings. By the mid-twentieth century the only one remaining re-branded itself as Ohio Yearly Meeting (Conservative).

In the twentieth century yearly meetings in the United States and Canada began to cluster together in larger groups that reflected their theological preferences. Two of them are Friends General Conference (FGC) and Conservative Friends (C). Both have traditional unprogrammed silent, waiting worship. The former is quite liberal in its theology, welcoming a wide diversity of beliefs and non-beliefs while the latter is strongly Christian.

Cleveland Meeting began as a worship group in the 1920s on the Western Reserve University campus. It included Friends from several of the branches of Quakers in the U.S. Eventually it was taken under the wing of the American Friends Service Committee (AFSC) which set up a committee to maintain contact with the new worship groups that were forming around the country, often on college campuses. When the Friends World Committee for Consultation (FWCC) was formed in 1937 the AFSC turned over the care of these new meetings to FWCC. Sometime in the early 1960s FWCC began to encourage these unaffiliated meetings and worship groups to form themselves into yearly meetings.

For some time there had been a loose association of new meetings in the Lake Erie area: western Pennsylvania, northern and eastern Ohio, northern West Virginia, and southern Michigan. There was also an active committee of visitation that circulated among the Ohio (Conservative) and new, more liberal campus meetings. As early as 1933 there was a Salem Quarterly Meeting (of OYM) minute describing favorably the previous three years of visitation. Many Friends in Cleveland participated in and developed close ties with Friends in both groups and did not want to be drawn into the old divisions. When the time came to decide whether to ask for affiliation with Ohio YM (C) or the newly forming Lake Erie YM and Association (FGC), Cleveland Meeting in 1965 chose to do both. It was accepted by both as a dual-affiliation member.

Cleveland Meeting, as a member of Ohio Yearly Meeting (C) was thereupon a member of Salem Quarter of Ohio YM and also of its Salem Quarter M&O and Ohio YM M&O. Salem Quarter then consisted of Cleveland, Middleton, Salem, Upper Springfield, and Winona Monthly Meetings.

In addition, Cleveland Meeting was a part of the much newer and less formal Lake Erie Yearly Meeting and Association that had no quarterly meeting in Ohio (there was one in Michigan), although there was a yearly meeting M&O committee. Additional meetings were in the process of joining LEYMA. In time Lake Erie dropped the "and Association".

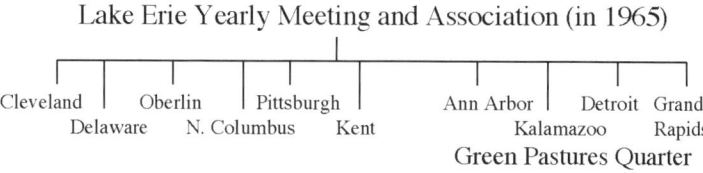

Lake Erie Yearly Meeting and Association (in 1965)

Cleveland, Oberlin, Pittsburgh, Ann Arbor, Detroit, Grand Rapids
Delaware, N. Columbus, Kent, Kalamazoo
Green Pastures Quarter

Although it was not always easy, and some individuals were only active in one yearly meeting or the other, not both, dual affiliation with two different branches of the Religious Society of Friends was enriching. There were wonderful treasures as well as glaring inadequacies in both groups. For some years Cleveland Friends functioned as a bridge, leavening each yearly meeting with some of the yeast from the other. While this was not always appreciated or understood by all, on balance it was useful and productive of growth.

There is one other topic that should be mentioned, especially for the benefit of any non-Friends who might read this account. Friends decisions are made through a corporate seeking of God's will for the group. There are no votes. When there is not unity on a sense of Divine Guidance, Friends wait. Our assumption is that God is present in our midst and will guide us so that we will be able to make decisions that bring us into closer harmony with Divine love. Since none of us has the exclusive ear to God's voice, we need to listen tenderly and respectfully to each other's listening, groping, and growing. But we are human and we do not always remember. Our egos, fears, and personal agendas drown out the still small voice.

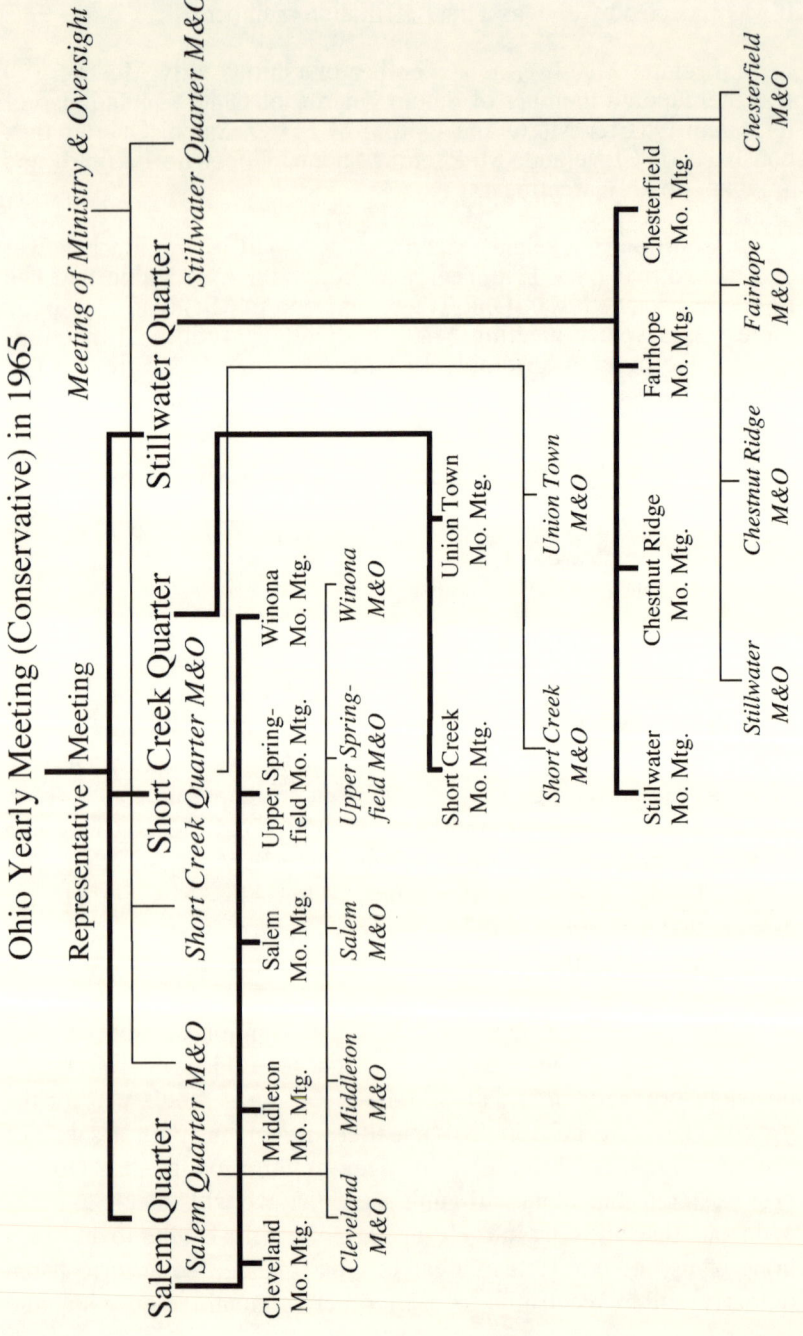

And yet, month after month we come together with a sense of adventure. Perhaps at this meeting we will fall into the presence of the living God, in which we experience deep and wordless unity. This is not to be confused with uniformity. It is a deep inward knowing, shared by all those present, that we are held by God. The decision as to a particular item of business becomes clear. Having once experienced this, we keep returning to meeting for business, like thirsty travellers to a well, hoping for another drink. It doesn't happen very often for us.

What follows is the chronicle not only of how the difficult but rich relationship with Ohio Yearly Meeting was ended, but more importantly, how Cleveland Friends Meeting reached clarity on what it felt called to do in regard to same sex relationships. Finding ourselves in unity in the Presence, then trying with varying degrees of faithfulness to act upon that unity, has been a touchstone for us. We record this so that those who have joined Cleveland Meeting more recently will have some small taste of our experience.

Marty Grundy
Cleveland Heights, 2010

1984-1985

The first notice of the issue of same-sex relationships taken by Cleveland Meeting for which we have documentation occurred in 1984 at a time when the meeting was generally focussed on sanctuary for Salvadorans and meeting finances in a time of rapid inflation.

From Monthly Meeting minutes, 9/30/1984:
Tom Holland asked for feedback on two matters. He and Ministry and Oversight would like suggestions for ways to begin discussion within the meeting of alternative lifestyles—forums, readings, midweek groups, etc. He would also like to hear from others who are concerned with making fuller use of career and vocation as ways of being of service to God and expressing the Light as we experience it.

Bill Shea and Erma Shea, Co-Clerks
Kathy Soltis, Assistant Clerk

From Monthly Meeting minutes, 10/28/1984:
Tom Holland then gave the Ministry and Oversight Committee report. He reminded Friends that M&O is seeking to promote fuller discussion of alternative lifestyles among Friends, to the end of increasing knowledge and understanding of all human relationships, including homosexuality. He recommended the following publications (and will make a reading list available): "Purple Balloons on Market Street" (*Friends Journal*, 11/1/84); *Toward a Quaker View of Sex* (booklet); *Is the Homosexual My Neighbor?*; *The Mendola Report*; and *Living with Oneself and Others* (Quaker booklet). See Tom to borrow any of these. He needs feedback on the way Friends want to proceed, particularly in order to include in the discussion those who are not necessarily close to this issue.

Bill Shea and Erma Shea, Co-Clerks
Kathy Soltis, Assistant Clerk

From Monthly Meeting minutes, 11/25/1984:
Tom Holland gave the Ministry and Oversight report. He is compiling a reading list on human relationships and homosexuality. A book shelf in the meeting room is available for reading material on those subjects.

Bill Shea and Erma Shea, Co-Clerks
Ruth-Maria P. Brutz [recording clerk for the day]

From Monthly Meeting minutes, 12/30/1984:
Tom Holland reported for M&O that in preparation for meaningful participation in the Friends for Lesbian and Gay Concerns conference in Cleveland in February, two meetings will be

held in January. The first will involve the FLGC program-planning committee, M&O, and other Cleveland Friends who are interested. It will take place after meeting on January 13. Participants will brainstorm on ways in which our two groups can share in activities.

The second meeting will take place at 7:00 p.m. on January 20 and will be an informal discussion on human relations and sexuality. We seek to understand the issue of homosexuality in a larger context and educate ourselves further. All are welcome at both meetings.

Bill Shea and Erma Shea, Co-Clerks
Kathy Soltis, Assistant Clerk

From Monthly Meeting minutes, 1/27/1985:

Nancy Reeves and Lynn Clark submitted an additional request on behalf of Friends for Lesbian and Gay Concerns. They wished to use the meeting house on Friday night, February 15, and Sunday night, February 17, for social activities related to the FLGC conference. The request was approved, with the usual rules regarding alcohol, smoking, and so forth applying. FLGC will make two attenders' badges available to people from the meeting. The exact arrangements for sharing the badges will be left open and worked out as needed. There will be partial fees for specific activities including Elizabeth Watson's talk.

Tom Holland presented the half-yearly report for the Ministry and Oversight Committee. He listed the following projects and concerns: small support groups and clearness committees for individual Friends, education and planning in preparation for the FLGC conference, pre-meeting discussions, discussions and presentations on Quakerism for outside groups, work with the Peace Committee in connection with the Hunger Center. Tom emphasized that Friends who are aware of needs and concerns that M&O might help to address should feel free to speak with a committee member—the door is open. (Members are Tom Holland – convener, Erma Shea, Marty Grundy, Nancy Reeves, Joe Purvis, Brigitte Streeter, and Kathy Soltis.)

Bill Shea and Erma Shea, Co-Clerks
Kathy Soltis, Assistant Clerk

Letter to Cleveland Friends Meeting
Dear Friends:

Greetings from the Planning Committee for the Friends for Lesbian and Gay Concerns Midwinter Gathering. We appreciate the loving support and assistance which has been given to us as we struggle with the seemingly endless details of bringing the FLGC Conference to Cleveland.

In the spirit of fellowship we would like to ask for your continuing love and support and the few things listed below:

1. Use of the Meeting House on Friday, February 15, from 6:00 pm until 10:00 pm for registration and fellowship. We do not anticipate a large crowd for Friday evening as many of those coming in will be trying to find their housing accommodations for the evening.

2. Use of the Meeting House on Sunday, February 17, from 10:00 pm until 1:00 am for a dance and fellowship. Because this is the last evening of the conference and some attenders will be leaving to go home we do not anticipate a large crowd.

3. We would like to ask permission to house up to ten attenders at the Meeting House during the conference weekend. We need a space near the Church of the Covenant for persons who will be arriving late Friday night. We will try to house members who are below the age of 22 years and will not be travelling to any local entertainment late in the evenings.

We have discussed the above with Lois and Tony Edgerton and John Perera and they have no objections.

Our only other need at this time remains housing. Many of the meeting members have graciously offered their homes and we are continuing to seek out beds and floor spaces as the registrations came in.

We wish to repeat our invitation to members of the Cleveland Meeting to join us for the conference. Either Nancy or I can provide listings of the workshops and the speakers and the complete schedule of the weekend. We all look forward to sharing worship with the Meeting an First Day, Second Month.

On behalf of the Planning Committee,

Lynn Clark and Nancy Reeves

From the February 1985 *Tatler*:

Ministry and Oversight prepared a reading list on human relationships, including homosexuality. An opportunity for sharing and exploring this area of our lives was held on Sunday, Feb. 2

Meeting on our Concern for Human Relationships

Under the guidance of Ministry and Oversight Committee, 25 people gathered to talk about matters very close to the heart and spirit for each of us. There was the beginning of some real sharing among people of many ages, backgrounds, experiences, and beliefs. Without feeling the need or readiness to come to any conclusions, we knew that we had made an important step in the direction of learning and looking more deeply together. We heard different voices speak about such things as the values of celibacy; the nurture of relationships which assist a person in growth; the need for a sense of rightness, Grace, looking for the Light in all relationships; the integration of sexuality with religion and all of life; the prevalence of homophobia in our society; and the need for Friends to try to find God's will in the way we see and treat each other. We raised such questions as: can we support heterosexuals and homosexuals so that they can grow and develop and more fully serve God? What is "natural" for our spiritually reborn lives? Is it right for us to speak of homosexuals as sick, or sinners, or to make them feel wrong, or miserable? How would Jesus have us live? Some people expressed the hope that we will continue this sharing and searching at another time.

From the May 1985 *Tatler*:

Cleveland Monthly Meeting of Friends received a letter from Geoffrey Kaiser containing two proposals to the Philadelphia Yearly Meeting and a minute from Unami Monthly Meeting regarding same sex marriage. Geoffrey Kaiser is a member of Unami Monthly Meeting who attended the FLGC [Friends for Gay and Lesbian Concerns] Midwinter Gathering held here in February.

The first proposal is that the Philadelphia Yearly Meeting consider the change of laws regarding marriage to extend the option of marriage to lesbian and gay couples. The second proposal is that the Philadelphia Yearly Meeting offer a Celebration of Commitment to lesbian and gay couples. This Celebration of Commitment will follow the guidelines for marriage set forth in the Philadelphia Yearly Meeting Faith and Practice.

The minute from Unami Monthly Meeting announced their intent to offer to all couples, both heterosexual and homosexual, a Celebration of Commitment. The reason for only offering such a Celebration, rather than marriage, is their feeling that it is wrong to offer different options to couples based on whether they are same sex or mixed sex. Since same sex couples cannot legally be married, Unami will not offer the option of marriage to any couples.

Ministry and Oversight has responded to this letter. The letter will be posted in the Meeting House and is available for reading or response from Nancy Reeves.

May 9, 1985

Box 222 Sumneytown, PA 18084
Dear Geoffrey Kaiser:

In preparation for the FLGC conference held here in Feb., the Ministry and Oversight Committee prepared a reading list and held a discussion on the topic: "Human Relations, Homosexuality". The meeting's discussion explored the wide range of opinions that are present today regarding this topic. These various opinions are maintained within our meeting community.

Your letter and the Minutes were read by the members of Ministry and Oversight and the following opinions were expressed:

We would support the issue of discrimination as we oppose discrimination of characteristics of people irrelevant to social circumstance.

We would appoint a committee to meet with the couple, but acknowledge there is much distance between members in the meeting regarding approval for marriage. One member feels marriage is a Holy Sacrament, ordained by God, only for two people of opposite sex. One member (was on the planning committee for FLGC) prefers Celebration of Marriage, rather than Celebration of Commitment.

For M.&O. Your Friend,

Erma Shea

Excerpt from the Ministry and Oversight Committee's Annual Report, Fifth Month, 1985

The national conference of Friends for Gay and Lesbian Concerns here last winter stimulated consideration of our human relationships. The Committee contributed to this process through collections of reading materials as well as group discussions. The preparations as well as the conference itself contributed to an increase in tenderness and respect for one another in all our variety.

1986-1987

From Monthly Meeting minutes, 7/27/1986:

A letter from Nancy Reeves and Lynn Clark declaring their intention to request marriage under the care of the meeting was read. Before they do this, however, they request that the meeting appoint a large, diverse committee to consider the issue of same-sex marriage and bring a recommendation to monthly meeting. Quentin Quereau and Marty Grundy will clerk this committee; all who would like to serve on it should speak to Quentin and Marty, who will also recruit Friends so as to ensure that a broad spectrum of opinion is represented. It is understood that this will be a difficult task, involving tender loving sharing, learning how to present highly emotionally charged feelings in a way that can be sensitively and lovingly heard and responded to. Most important, however, is that each member of the committee be open to God's leading. We hope that this committee can become a prototype of the way our meeting goes about dealing with difficult issues.

Judy Purvis, Clerk
Katherine Soltis, Recording Clerk

The committee clerks met to prayerfully consider who might best serve on this committee. Over the next days, without the clerks saying anything, everyone the clerks had listed came forward volunteering to be on it. It was humbling and encouraging that the process was starting out with such Divine assistance. The committee met every Monday from 10/13/1986 to 12/15/1986, and again on 1/12/1987, 1/26/1987. No official minutes were kept of these meetings.

In time we reached an impasse and the co-facilitators met 2/26/1987 to discuss where we might go from here. We agreed that more of the way things went the last few sessions would be counter-productive, creating more hurt, and not getting any closer to unity.

Minute prepared by the co-facilitators
approved by Monthly Meeting.

After four months of prayerful sharing and discussion, the committee to consider the issue of same sex marriage has proved conclusively what it knew at the beginning: that when there is a highly emotional issue on which Friends hold strong and diametrically opposed views, it is humanly impossible to reach consensus. However, we affirm our faith in God's unchanging love, and believe that if we could lay aside our personal agendas we would be enabled to see God's will for Cleveland Meeting on this issue.

Quentin Quereau & Marty Grundy, Co-facilitators

The last session was held on 4/20/1987.

In the meantime there was some activity within **Ohio Yearly Meeting (Conservative)** *around the issue of homosexuality and same-sex marriage.*

Our member who attended Salem Quarterly Meeting for Ministry and Oversight reported to Cleveland **Monthly Meeting, 2/22/1987**, *that there is appreciation for Cleveland's diversity, they will pray for us, and ask us to pray for them.*

In **Monthly Meeting, 3/29/1987** *a letter was read from Ohio YM Representative Meeting in which they noted our same sex marriage committee and will pray for us.*

The clerk of Cleveland Meeting received a minute from Salem Quarterly Meeting of Ministry and Oversight. It was approved at a special session of the Quarterly Meeting of Ministry and Oversight that was called so hastily nobody from Cleveland could attend. The clerk of the Quarterly Meeting of Ministry and Oversight did not contact either of the convenors of our special committee, our clerk of M&O, or Cleveland Meeting's clerk ahead of time to enquire what was going on in Cleveland. They adopted a minute, the heart of which was an unequivocal statement that the Heavenly Father had set up the family unit as "man & woman joined in marriage, and children", and that they "cannot endorse any other marital combination procedures within any of our subordinate meetings".

The OYM Book of Discipline states that "A Meeting for Ministry and Oversight shall not interfere with the affairs of any meeting for business, but it may present any subject which it feels should be considered therein."

From Monthly Meeting minutes, 4/26/1987
11. The Committee to Consider the Question of Same-Sex Marriage has approved a minute but is not yet ready to report back to monthly meeting because it wishes to prepare a report on the questions with which we dealt and the prayerful process by which we proceeded. The Committee wants to present both things at a monthly meeting in which there will be adequate time for discussion.

Marty Grundy, Clerk
Katherine Soltis, Recording Clerk

From Annual Meeting minutes, 5/31/1987:
4. After reviewing the chronology of minutes and meetings concerning the issue of same sex marriage as dealt with by Salem Quarterly Meeting of Ministry and Oversight, OYM Representative Meeting, and our own Ministry and Oversight Committee, we agreed to postpone further discussion to Seventh Month's meeting.

Marty Grundy, Clerk
Katherine Soltis, Recording Clerk

Ministry and Oversight Committee's message to Annual Meeting, held 5/31/1987, mostly concerned this issue.

Excerpt from the 5/31/1987 Cleveland Meeting State of the Meeting Report
This year we have been considering the issue of same-sex marriage. We named a large, broadly-based committee to consider it and bring a recommendation to monthly meeting. The committee met once a week for over five months. During the process it had to deal with fundamental, underlying issues like what we mean by the sense of the meeting and how it "happens"; whether we really believe in the possibility of continuing revelation and how new truths are received from God; our understanding of the Bible and its interpretation; how we are moved by the Holy Spirit and how we differentiate between divine 'nudges' and our own emotional or psychological or intellectual impulses, needs, or ideas; what we mean by 'expectant waiting'. In addition, the committee explored what we mean by 'marriage' and how that differs from any other loving relationship. The committee has not been able to reach consensus, but expects to report to monthly meeting in July.

Marty Grundy, Clerk

From Monthly Meeting minutes, 7/26/1987:
7. After meeting together for five months, the committee formed to consider and bring forth a recommendation concerning same-sex marriage has not reached consensus either for or against oversight of such a marriage. Therefore we are laying aside our human process of weekly committee meetings—and, with the full

Meeting, we are entering a period of open and expectant waiting. We depend upon God's work continuing within us and the right path opening.

The report of the process was also read, and both were accepted with thanks for work of the committee. It was noted the committee had also discussed various alternative celebrations of commitment, and the Meeting could do further such exploration. This is a time of healing our hurts and anger. We ask Ministry and Oversight to consider (1) how to assist the process of healing, (2) possibilities to explore the question with Salem Quarter, (3) what do we mean by 'open and expectant waiting', (4) ways to safeguard Quaker process during all of this, and (5) providing outside speakers and/or resources to help the Meeting deepen its understanding of this issue and of how to find and follow God's will. We also ask the committee to make available through the library the variety of written materials used, plus others which may become available.

Marty Grundy, Clerk
Katherine Soltis, Recording Clerk

Report of the Committee to Consider and Bring Forth a Recommendation Concerning the Issue of Same Sex Marriage, 7/26/1987

The idea for this committee arose in a small gathered meeting, as the way to bring the issue to the attention of Friends separate from the request for oversight of a same sex marriage which would be brought at a later time. The committee was approved by Monthly Meeting. The members either volunteered or were appointed in such a way as to ensure a broad base of widely diverse initial views, and so as to have only one person from any given couple. It seemed to be confirmation of the initial gathered meeting that all those who later volunteered were people whose names had come up that evening.

The group met nearly every Monday evening for almost 5 months. Sometimes it held a discussion. More often it used a Quaker Dialogue format in which each person spoke out of the silence and there was no challenge to or discussion of any contribution.

We began by sharing times we had experienced a real consensus or a God-centered meeting for business. Quaker procedure is built on the expectation that "where two or three are gathered" in His name, Christ will be in their midst, and He will provide the leadership. However, some in the group were not sure that it is possible nowadays for a group to really find God's will.

The group generated the following questions, with which we wrestled for a considerable number of evenings:

What do you think of when you hear the word "marriage"?
Where do we get our ideas about marriage? of what it could or should be?
What are the elements which make a "good" marriage?

What is the purpose of marriage?
How has the institution of marriage evolved over the years?
Why is it important to be married in a religious ceremony?
What do "divine assistance", love, and faithfulness mean in the Quaker marriage promise?

We explored Friends' understanding of the Bible: that while it was written under the inspiration of the Holy Spirit, it must also be read under that same Spirit in order to fully comprehend it. We looked at very different interpretations of several passages.

In order to arrive at consensus on a difficult issue, it is necessary to step out of individualism and into a "community" mode. As we shared our understanding on the above questions we were also building up the trust and willingness to listen and share even more deeply, which we hoped would eventually get us to the point where we could be open to God's leading. We were aware that the Friends' process could be short-circuited if *any* of us assumed that our position was the "correct" one. We all had to let go, while we entered into a joint experience of God's guiding presence.

As the process continued over the weeks, there were three major issues on which we spent a fair amount of time. First was the spiritual or religious dimension of marriage. Second was sorting out the difference between marriage and any other committed relationship. Third was our physical bodies as gifts from God, and understanding how we use and enjoy our sexuality.

Gradually the group got deeper and deeper into the emotional areas surrounding the subject. We explored what it feels like to be the victim of homophobia. We learned of the repugnance some feel about anal intercourse.

After five months of prayerful sharing and discussion, the committee to consider the issue of same sex marriage has proved conclusively what it suspected at the beginning: that when there is a highly emotional issue on which Friends hold strong and widely divergent views, it is very difficult to reach consensus using only the human tools of logic, persuasion, emotion or reason. However, we affirm our faith in God's unchanging love, and believe that if we could lay aside our personal agendas and gather in the faith that Christ is come to lead His people, we would be enabled to see God's will for Cleveland Meeting on this issue.

A minute was adopted affirming that we had failed to agree to approve or disapprove of sanctioning same sex marriage. In Fourth Month the Salem Quarterly Meeting of Ministry and Oversight, in the absence of Friends from Cleveland, minuted an unequivocal statement that the Heavenly Father had set up the family unit as "man & woman joined in marriage, and children," and that it "cannot endorse any other marital combination procedures within any of our subordinate meetings." Cleveland Meeting's Ministry and Oversight Committee formally requested that a few lines be appended to the minute stating that we had not been part of its acceptance and were not in unity with it.

Marty Grundy and Quentin Quereau, Co-Clerks

From Monthly Meeting, 8/30/1987:
 4. In response to the concerns laid on Ministry and Oversight last month around the issue of same sex marriage, the Committee recommends that there needs to be a time for healing and therefore nothing formal is planned for now.

Marty Grundy, Clerk
Katherine Soltis and Carolyn Rudd, Co-Assistant Clerks

There was a break for well over a year.

1988

From Monthly Meeting minutes, 7/31/1988 [23 people present]:
 8. A request was received from the Ohio Friends for Lesbian and Gay Concerns asking to hold a gathering in the meeting house on September 10-11. Friends approved this use of our space.

Marty Grundy and Nancy Reeves, Co-Clerks
Carolyn Rudd, Assistant Clerk

1989

From Monthly Meeting minutes, 4/30/1989:
 12. We received a request for marriage under the care of the meeting from William Beasley and Elizabeth Spraker. We ask that Jody Taslitz, Marty Grundy, Tom Cooke, and others appointed by Ministry and Oversight serve as their clearness committee.

 13. As we consider this marriage we note that we have not yet been able to reach clearness on the issue of same-gender marriage under the care of the Cleveland Meeting. We ask Ministry and Oversight Committee to explore and suggest a method by which the Meeting can begin to reexamine this issue.

 14. A letter from Winona Monthly Meeting regarding an addition to the 4th query from OYM was read. The letter references the 11th month Representative Meeting but has no heading or date. It was mailed April 3, 1989. They suggest the following: "Are we opposed to fornication, adultery, homosexuality, pornography, and child abuse?" This meeting feels a strong concern about this addition to the query. Carolyn Rudd will check with Rose Sidwell to see if the letter was approved by Winona Monthly Meeting. We ask that the letter be printed in the *Tatler* and copies of it be circulated within the Cleveland Friends Meeting, with an

explanation of its origin. In order that we may make a loving and well considered response we ask that the Ministry and Oversight Committee prepare a draft and bring it for consideration at our May Meeting for Business. We recognize and affirm the love of family values from which this letter seems to grow and wish to respond constructively to the fear of losing them. So that we may be prepared to respond to the issue if it arises prior to our approval of a response, we minute our strong disapproval of the proposed addition.

Nancy Reeves, Co-clerk
Carolyn Rudd, Assistant Clerk

From Annual Meeting minutes, 5/21/1989:

2. The Clearness Committee for William Beasley and Elizabeth Spraker unanimously and enthusiastically recommends that the couple be cleared to proceed with their marriage. The Meeting approves. An Oversight Committee was named consisting of Marty Grundy, Jody Taslitz, Kathy Soltis, and if they will serve, Tom Cooke, Ted Wood, and Kathy Wood.

13. We have heard the message from the clerk of Ministry and Oversight. The Committee proposes to hold a mid-week meeting for worship twice a month to seek God's will for Cleveland Meeting on the themes of homosexuality, same sex marriage, heterosexual marriage, sexuality, and our relations with our two yearly meetings. We approve; a time and dates will be arranged later."

Nancy Reeves and Marty Grundy, Co-Clerks
Carolyn Rudd, Assistant Clerk

Response of Cleveland Meeting to Ohio YM Representative Meeting Concerning Homosexuality, 5/21/1989

For some time Cleveland Meeting has been struggling with the issue of homosexuality and same sex marriage. Beginning in the fall of 1986 a large, diverse committee met to consider it. In Seventh Month 1987 the Meeting minuted that we had "not reached a consensus either for or against oversight of such a marriage. Therefore we are laying aside our human process of weekly committee meetings and . . . entering a period of open and expectant waiting. We depend upon God's work continuing within us and the right path opening."

We thank Representative Meeting for reminding us that more work needs to be done. We know that homosexuality raises strong feelings in this country. People argue for or against it using moral, legal, Biblical, historical, psychological, biological, and social arguments. But we know that for us, as a monthly meeting of the Religious Society of Friends, we cannot reach a decision using any of these arguments as definitive. We must, as Friends, learn from Christ who is come to teach us, his people, himself.

We affirm that the letter killeth but the Spirit giveth life. [2 Corinth. 3:6] As Christian Quakers we believe that we are called to obey Christ wholeheartedly, wherever the Spirit leads. We gather in silence expecting God's guidance, and striving to bring ourselves, individually and corporately, to a clear discernment of what God is teaching us to do. We acknowledge that we are told to work out our own salvation, with fear and trembling, by listening to and obeying the Inward Christ. As Friends we have faith that the Light, the Word that was in the beginning before words were, is working in us, making us willing and able to obey God's purpose. [Phil. 2:12-13]

Therefore, on the recommendation of our Ministry and Oversight Committee, Cleveland Friends have agreed to begin holding midweek meetings for worship twice a month. We believe that if we are able to lay aside our own personal hopes and fears, to admit humbly our weaknesses, to invite the Light to search our inmost hearts, we believe that if we come with openness and stillness, and pray for direction, that Christ will be among us, and will instruct us, and empower us to obey whatever difficult things he asks of us. We trust that the Yearly Meeting will affirm this process and will allow us time to complete it.

From Monthly Meeting minutes, 9/24/1989:

8. Ministry and Oversight proposes that, in addition to the twice-monthly called meetings for worship, a clearness committee be formed to labor with those who have strongly held opinions about homosexuality, same-gender marriage, and our relationships with our two yearly meetings. We approve the names of Jody Taslitz, David Male, Marty Grundy, and Carolyn Rudd if she is willing when she returns from vacation; we recommend that all who have suggestions about a possible way forward submit them in writing to the clearness committee. Friends who have strong opinions or reservations or misgivings about the pros and cons of solemnizing such a relationship should make themselves known to the committee. It is hoped that this committee will help us discern God's truth for us which it cannot do if it does not reach all who have concerns. We ask all F/friends to pray for the necessary clarity to see beyond our personal views.

Carol Conti-Entin and Nancy Reeves, Co-Clerks
Recording Clerk for the Day

This clearness committee was unofficially and irreverently nick-named the Polish Committee because it sought to listen to all Friends on opposing poles.

1990

From Monthly Meeting minutes, 1/28/1990:
9. The Interim Report of the Ministry and Oversight Committee was read. We ask the committee to do what it needs to ensure that the clearness committee for same-gender marriage concerns can carry out its work. . . .

Carol Conti-Entin and Nancy Reeves, Co-Clerks
Carolyn Rudd, Assistant Clerk

Excerpt from the Interim Report of Ministry and Oversight Committee, 1/1990

At annual meeting in May Ministry and Oversight proposed that we start a bi-monthly called meeting for worship with concern for same-sex marriage. The Meeting's previous attempts at finding clearness on the subject hadn't worked and we hoped this would. Annual meeting approved with an expanded concern list—adding marriage and our relationship with our yearly meetings. The called meetings were fruitful to some people and frustrating to others. Some Meeting members felt compelled to attend so their viewpoints wouldn't be ignored. In September Ministry and Oversight formed a clearness committee to work with the people who had strong beliefs on the matter. The number of people attending the called meetings was shrinking and Ministry and Oversight recommended to the December meeting for business that the Meeting lay down the called meetings. We thought that the called meetings were a finished phase in a process that was not yet finished. The discussions that didn't find a way led us to a clearness committee. Whether this is God's mysterious process or us covering our ears and muffling a clear call is unknown. Obviously, finding God's leading for Cleveland Meeting on this is unfinished business.

Ruth Brutz, clerk of Ministry and Oversight Committee

Interim Report of the Clearness Committee

The committee approved by monthly meeting on 9/24/1989 to "labor with those who have strongly held opinions about homosexuality, same-gender marriage, and our relationships with our two yearly meetings" is in the process of meeting with those who have asked to meet and with those whose views are widely known. As we have considered this process we are reminded of Arlene Kelly's advice when Central Philadelphia Meeting was struggling with its difficult situation regarding the homeless man named "Jealous". Central Philadelphia made it clear to all in the meeting that the only way Quaker process can work is if everyone is involved and is present, allowing the Spirit to work within the gathered group. Therefore Friends who absented themselves from the ongoing process but came to the final decision-reaching meeting were not prevented from speaking but their views were not given the weight of those who had been part of the process.

Our committee concurs with Central Philadelphia, and feels that it should be understood by everyone in Cleveland Meeting that only those who have been participating in our long, sometimes painful, process will carry weight when a final decision is reached.

From Monthly Meeting minutes, 3/25/1990:

9. Announcements reminded us of the business awaiting us next month and of the necessity for participating now in the clearness committee process. . . . Any persons who have strong feelings about a possible outcome and who wish to take part when the clearness committee proposes a minute to meeting for business need to have spoken with the clearness committee by mid-April. Persons who have any doubt that the committee knows of their feelings should contact Marty Grundy or David Male.

Carol Conti-Entin and Nancy Reeves, Co-Clerks
Carolyn Rudd, Assistant Clerk

From Monthly Meeting minutes, 4/29/1990:

8. David Male read a proposed statement on homosexuality from Cleveland Meeting to Ohio Yearly Meeting which consisted of a full explanation of our process and experience and a summary statement as our response to the request from Ohio Yearly Meeting's Representative Meeting for a statement on homosexuality. We are all aware of and grateful for the extensive and prayerful work of the clearness committee. We approved sending the entire report to Representative Meeting.

Carol Conti-Entin, Co-Clerk
Carolyn Rudd, Assistant Clerk

Cleveland Meeting's Statement on Homosexuality approved by Monthly Meeting 4/29/1990

We have been aware, to a greater or lesser extent, of lesbian and gay Friends worshipping with us over the years. In 1986 we were asked to consider whether we would be willing to oversee a marriage between two people of the same gender. The Meeting named a broadly-based committee of sixteen people, which met once a week for over six months, considering many aspects of marriage, sexuality, the Bible, and how we hear God. In Seventh Month 1987 the Meeting minuted that we had "not reached a consensus either for or against oversight of such a marriage. Therefore we are laying aside our human process of weekly committee meetings and . . . entering a period of open and expectant waiting. We depend upon God's work continuing within us and the right path opening."

In Eleventh Month 1988 Ohio Yearly Meeting's Representative Meeting asked each monthly meeting to submit a statement on homosexuality. It was clear that Cleveland Meeting did not have unity. So in Fifth Month 1989 we began a process of bi-weekly called meetings for worship seeking God's will for our Meeting. After seven months, attendance had dwindled and it appeared that the Meeting was no longer wholeheartedly involved in the process, so it was laid down. Next, the Meeting approved in Ninth month the appointment by Ministry and Oversight of a small committee to labor with those who have strongly-held opinions, seeking to find a place where we unite. The committee met with at least a dozen people and submitted this report:

Cleveland Meeting can share these experiences and understandings which are based on our common desire for spiritual growth for all Friends, and our determination not to condone that which is evil nor condemn that which is not.

- It is our experience that two women have told us they consider themselves married in the sight of God;

- It is our experience that we love each of them as part of our meeting community and pray that they, like all of us, find and follow God's purpose for their lives;

- It is our experience that Cleveland Friends have testified to the fruits of the Spirit in lesbians and gays with whom we have worshipped;

- It is our experience that Friends have testified that the deepest, most gathered meetings for worship that they have experienced are under Ohio Yearly Meeting and Friends for Lesbian and Gay Concerns;

- It is our experience that there are people who are gay or lesbian who find the best way for them to experience corporately the living presence of Christ's Spirit is through unprogrammed meetings for worship. We do not feel we should deny people this opportunity to worship because they are homosexual.

We affirm the advice of Gamaliel: "Leave them alone! If what they have planned and done is of human origin, it will disappear, but if it comes from God, you cannot possibly defeat them. You could find yourselves fighting against God!" [Acts 5:38-39]

This whole process has taught us a lot. We have often felt the guidance of God. We note that God has not raised up a prophet in our meeting, to give us a statement for all Friends and for all times. We cannot, therefore, answer this question for others. We have come to see that we here in Cleveland Meeting are to bring it out from the dark and put it on a lampstand to allow the Light to work with it in each person's heart. It is there that God has written God's desire, and with the guidance of the Spirit, each of us can find it for ourselves. This is the only way we know for God's Truth to prevail.

This is our statement to Ohio Yearly Meeting:

We affirm that it is God who judges, not us. We are commanded to love one another. Cleveland Meeting takes this stand: we are not pro-homosexual nor are we anti-homosexual. We are Friends. We welcome all who seek Truth and want to worship

Christ who, we believe, is come to teach us himself. We affirm the one, Christ Jesus, who speaks to each of us in the condition in which we find ourselves. We have faith that God sees the unity underlying our seeming diversity, and trust that God can lead us into all Truth. Evil works in darkness and confusion; in the Light and love of Christ, Truth will prevail. We leave ourselves in God's hands.

From Cleveland's Annual Meeting minutes, 5/20/1990:

1. We have heard with thanks the report from Ruth Brutz, the Clerk of Ministry and Oversight Committee.

2. It was brought to our attention that the Statement on Homosexuality which was approved last month contained a slight wording difference from the version which appeared in the *Tatler*. We approve the following wording for the final sentence in the version which will be brought to OYM Representative Meeting next week: "We leave ourselves in God's hands." We note that the matter is far from settled within other Meetings of OYM. Carol Conti-Entin will check to be sure that copies of Cleveland's statement have been or will be sent to all monthly meetings within OYM.

Carol Conti-Entin and Nancy Reeves, Co-Clerks
Carolyn Rudd, Assistant Clerk

Excerpts from Ministry and Oversight Committee Report, 5/1990

This has been a year of change in Cleveland Meeting and the change is not over yet. Some of the currents in the Meeting are reflected in the minute on homosexuality and the process that brought about that minute. Last year's M & O Report to Annual Meeting proposed called mid-week meetings for worship with concern for same-sex marriage. The called meetings ended as attendance dwindled, and a clearness committee was formed. The clearness committee met with deeply concerned members and wrote a minute that accurately states where the meeting is right now. The minute doesn't pretend that we have had any leadings that we haven't had, or that we know more than we do.

Hearing the truth so plainly said is both comforting and squirm-inducing. To take a hard situation and look it straight in the eye brings inner peace. You may not like what you see, but at least you are wrestling with reality and not with delusion. . . .

When we started the called meetings with concern for same-sex marriage, we were waiting for a leading from God. When the leadings we had did not give us a definite yes or no we were able to accept that, and not ram false leadings down dissenting throats. Every concerned person had a chance to be part of the process, to bring their experience of God's love to the search for a way to handle a difficult situation. That we managed to do these things is

very encouraging. We must try to weave these vital threads into our handling of what God sets before us this year.
Ruth Brutz, Clerk of Ministry and Oversight Committee

1991

From Monthly Meeting minutes, 1/27/1991:

7. The Ministry and Oversight committee recommends that we name Nancy Reeves, Tom Cooke, and Lynn Clark as our representatives to the mid-winter gathering of FLGC. Approved. We look forward to hearing their report of the gathering.
Lois Edgerton, Clerk
Carol Conti-Entin, Assistant Clerk

From Monthly Meeting minutes, 3/31/1991:

1. Nancy Reeves and Tom Cooke reported on the 1991 Midwinter Gathering of Friends for Lesbian and Gay Concerns. We are thankful for the honest and hard-earned insights these our Friends bring us and our Meeting.
Lois Edgerton, Clerk
Carol Conti-Entin, Assistant Clerk

From the *Tatler*, Third Month 1991:
Midwinter Gathering of FLGC

"Gay Gifts: Sparking New Lights Among Friends". This was the theme of the 1991 Midwinter gathering of Friends for Lesbian and Gay Concerns. When I returned home my first thought about trying to make a report on the gathering to the Cleveland Meeting was, "New Lights, I can't even find the old Lights!"

The gathering was a difficult one for me. I was just past the worst of the flu, Emma was at the peak of it, and Lynn was on the verge of coming down with it. Because of job, car and money considerations we had to drive to Washington, D.C. after work Thursday and drive back immediately after the gathering ended at 2pm on Monday. It was the first time I have clerked a meeting since Emma was born and the first time since "stranger anxiety" appeared that Emma was around 150 "strangers". The overseers of FLGC had an extremely rough weekend. While not directly involved with the overseers' work, the clerks have a close enough relationship with the overseers that I felt some of what one overseer described as, "the seeds of Darkness which almost overcame" him.

I could not attend much of the weekend and what I did attend was stressful. Until last Sunday, two weeks after the gathering, I didn't feel that I had gained anything for myself that I could share with others.

While I was wallowing in my annoyance at the practice of replacing Meeting for Worship with Meeting for Business one First Day a month, I began to see a glimmer of new Light. I would like to share this spark with Cleveland Friends.

We had a particularly difficult Meeting for Worship with Attention to Business on Monday. Several Friends were uncomfortable using the word "darkness" in a negative context because of the racial connection it made for them. Others were uncomfortable because the "seeds of darkness" sounded too "fundamentalist". Still others were uncomfortable altering the words a Friend had used to describe his experience of what he had come in contact with. The overseers had come to the meeting asking for prayer and support in their work. One friend noted that our quibbles over words almost seemed to take precedence over the urgent request of the overseers for help. We kept coming close to an acceptable minute then diverging again and again.

The time we had set to end Meeting for Worship, which was to follow Meeting for Worship with Attention to Business, was 12:00. At 11:45 we still had one 30-minute item of business left to go. We put aside the last item (more about it later) and entered Meeting for Worship with Attention to Worship.

At lunch a Friend commented to me that the Meeting for Worship with Attention to Business had been so worshipful that she would not have minded if we had skipped the Meeting for Worship entirely. Last Sunday I thought again about why our Meetings for Worship with Attention to Business often feel so worshipful that one might not miss Meeting for Worship if it were skipped that day. When I am actively clerking I put all my energy into listening, both to the gathered meeting and to God. I strive to express the golden threads common to all the voices I hear, and to name those threads which are not yet part of the fabric. When I am not actively clerking I put my full attention to holding Peter Burkholder (my co-clerk) or Annie Frederickson (our recording clerk) in the Light as they strive to gather or record the sense of the meeting. As I glance out into the body of the meeting I see many individuals bathed in the Light as they worship completely and without reservation. Each of us in the meeting has a job to do, some of us to name, some to record, some to listen, some to hold in the Light. Each of us knows we cannot complete our task without God's help. When we claim our tasks and allow God to help us in their completion a very deep sense of worship occurs. Our final Meeting for Worship with Attention to Business was such a meeting. It was exhausting, but to quote the punch line of a story Jan Hoffman shared with us in her address to FGC at Oberlin, "Of course I'm burned out, when I am on fire with the Lord's work how can I help but burn out?"

The thoughts I've shared above are not new to me, but they are the stones which tumbled together to create the spark of new Light I received from the weekend.

Our last item of business at the final Meeting for Worship with Attention to Business at each gathering is supposed to be the writing of a closing minute. Friends share, under the discipline of business, their experience of the gathering. At the end of the sharing we worship while our recording clerk weaves these comments into a minute which captures the essence of the gathering. We struggled, at 11:45, to figure out how to take 30 minutes to write a closing minute, spend an hour in worship, and still end by noon. A suggestion was made that we move into Meeting for Worship and at the end of the meeting Annie could compose the closing minute. Her immediate reaction was to inquire, "When can the recording clerk be released to worship?"

I realize that my own feelings match what Annie seemed to be expressing. When I move from Meeting for Worship with Attention to Business to meeting for Worship, I feel released. I can "let down"; relax a bit.

I'm starting to wonder about that difference.

I wonder if it is right to feel released when I worship with attention to worship rather than business.

If each of us accepting our task and God's help in its completion is what makes doing business worshipful, I wonder what my task is during worship.

I wonder if I should feel "burned out" at the end of worship as I do at the end of business.

Most of all I wonder what Meeting for Worship would be like if I worked as hard at worship as I do at clerking, and everyone else worked that hard, too.

Nancy Reeves

From Monthly Meeting minutes, 4/28/1991:

7. Ministry and Oversight Committee has brought to us, with its approval, the following request: that Friends for Lesbian and Gay Concerns sponsor a Meeting for Worship and potluck on the second Sunday of each month. These gatherings would be under the care of the Ministry and Oversight Committee of Cleveland Meeting and would be open to all who wish to attend. Approved.

Lois Edgerton, Clerk
Carol Conti-Entin, Assistant Clerk

From Monthly Meeting minutes, 8/25/1991:

5. Request for use of the Meeting House from 3-6 pm on Saturday, Sept. 21 has come from Lynn Clark and Nancy Reeves, who are planning a worship service and party to celebrate their ten years of being together. Approved.

Lois Edgerton, Clerk
Carolyn Rudd, assistant clerk

1992

Letter from Ministry and Oversight Committee to Representative Meeting of Ohio Yearly Meeting, 5/10/1992

Dear Friends:

We would like to respond to two issues raised at the last Representative Meeting which were forwarded to the monthly meetings.

The first involves the minute by South West Yearly Meeting Friends Church. We feel strongly that we should not become involved in this issue. We understand that the proposal to restructure Friends United Meeting is for that group of Friends to decide, and they have minuted that it is not going to go forward. It seems like within the context of FUM controversies, South West Yearly Meeting is trying to keep open the issue of separation. We do not want to support such a move in any way. We support the recent efforts of our Yearly Meeting's Spiritual Action Committee to move closer in unity, to look for the things that unite us rather than those which divide us.

The second issue involves membership. Cleveland Meeting has begun a process of discussion of the meaning of membership and the ramifications of it. So far we have held five open meetings in the hour before meeting for worship. We have not yet completed the process. We hope that OYM will not move hastily on this issue before we have had a chance to arrive at a carefully considered minute.

In the meantime we would like to draw Friends' attention to Cleveland's category of "link member". This is a person who has moved out of town and can no longer participate in any meaningful way in the ongoing spiritual life of the meeting community. But such a person still has a love for the meeting and warm memories of their time with us. A "link member" does not bear financial or other responsibility toward the meeting, and does not count in the FWCC census figures. But they do maintain a tie with us, and receive mailings. It is completely voluntary. Such a category is somewhat like the associate membership William Taber has suggested. It may provide a way for the membership lists of meetings within OYM to more accurately reflect the true nature of its ongoing faith community. It could then be a list of those who feel responsible for the meeting and those for whom the meeting exercises care.

On behalf of Ministry and Oversight Committee of Cleveland Meeting,

Ruth Peck Brutz, Clerk

From the *Tatler*, 9/1992:
Homosexuality and Same-Gender Marriage

Since 1986 Cleveland Meeting has struggled, with varying degrees of intensity, with these issues. In 1990 Cleveland Friends Meeting accepted the following summary report . . . Ministry and

Oversight asks it these statements still reflect where Cleveland Friends are on these issues. The following queries seek to move the discussion towards an underlying, deeper unity:
 1. Do we share a faith in a God who loves each of us and all of us?
 2. Can we trust that God to bring us into loving unity with one another?

From Monthly Meeting 12/27/1992:
 4. Ministry and Oversight has written a minute to Cleveland Meeting that is printed in the 12th Month *Tatler*. They would appreciate any responses from the rest of the Meeting.

Lois Edgerton, Clerk
Betty B. Lake, Assistant Clerk

A Letter from Ministry and Oversight Committee to Cleveland Friends Meeting

We have been charged by God to engage in a deep testing of our faith in God and our love for one another. Shall we rise to the challenge or attempt to maintain a semi-friendly status-quo?

There are homosexuals among us. They tell us that this is who they are, not a choice they make. They deeply resent being told that what to them is an essential part of themselves is an abomination unto God. They are deeply hurt by members of our community who appear to withhold their love from them while claiming that God loves us all.

There are those among us who believe that while we are certainly taught to try to love everyone, the Bible states clearly that homosexual behavior is against God's will. They feel that honoring same-sex relationships would be honoring sin and they cannot do this.

There are others among us who don't know the Bible or who understand it differently. There are those who haven't thought much about homosexuality. Some don't see what the controversy is, others wish the problem would just go away. Some feel strongly what the solution should be and can't understand what's wrong with the rest of us who don't see it that way.

Is it possible that the Bible is wrong?

Is it possible that our understanding of the Bible is wrong?

Is it possible that one God has more than one truth?

Is it possible that we are so determined to have our own way that we are unwilling to earnestly ask God to reveal the Truth plainly to all of us?

Do we not believe that the Creator of heaven and earth is powerful enough to do that?

Can we please just try to love one another in the meantime?

Ministry and Oversight, 5/11/1992

1993

From the 1/1993 Tatler:
Message from Ministry and oversight Committee
Dear Friends,

M & O has received letters about same gender marriage, and though diverse feelings were expressed all of the letters reflect much thought and prayer. It seems to us that this issue and its underlying themes of unity in the midst of variety and peaceful conflict resolution need to be addressed openly by the meeting as a community. Within M & O we have gone from butting heads in disagreement to a feeling of unity in spite of differing opinions. We hope this type of growth can happen in the whole meeting.

Ruth Brutz, clerk of Ministry and Oversight Committee

The following is offered as a springboard to deep thought and discussion. It is not intended as a definitive statement.

For more than six years Cleveland Meeting has been engaged in a dialogue regarding same gender marriage. Sometimes it has seemed more like an exercise in head-butting. It has felt at times like a game in which one side, and only one side, can win while the other loses.

Ministry and Oversight Committee would like to invite Cleveland Meeting to shift the paradigm from a choice of two polar positions to a third way. This paradigm shift requires placing homosexuality in a different framework than the dichotomy of blessing or cursing the relationships.

Under the old covenant between God and humans, laws were written and interpreted and intended to cover every contingency. But understanding grows, conditions change, and individual situations demand special consideration. The written law was a trap which failed to bring people into right relationship with God. So God graciously gave us a new covenant, one in which the law was written on each person's heart. No longer were we to repeat the law over and over, to teach it to our children and neighbors. Now we were invited to look into our own hearts and see what God required of us. George Fox discovered that this law written on our heart was synonymous with Christ's Spirit within us which actively teaches and guides us in our daily lives.

When we are faced with a difficult issue, the new covenant calls us to see what the law written on our own heart is telling us. It does not call us to interpret what the law says in someone else's heart. Our task as a Religious Society of Friends is to encourage each individual to be passionately concerned to pay attention to the law in their own heart. We are not given the task of judging each other's hearts or what is found there. God has reserved the judging to God's self; we can be free to love one another. When Jesus defined who were his followers, his Friends, he said they were the people who followed his commands. In the very next breath he made it explicit: "and this is my command, that you love one another." Jesus did not say that we were to judge one another, condemn one another, and poke around in each other's heart to make sure others read their laws the way we think they should.

As a Religious Society with a beloved testimony of peace, we get uneasy and uncomfortable with conflict. We wonder if being in conflict with one another somehow means that we are not a peaceful people. But peace is not the absence of conflict. Peace lies beyond conflict. It is produced by the powerful and positive force of love, good will, and trust that God's power is over all. Conflict is often a by-product of growth and change. The question is not does the meeting experience conflict, but how does the meeting deal with it and get beyond it? Are we afraid to face conflict because we are secretly afraid that God's power is not "over all"? That God is not going to bring the solution that I desire? That we are hypocrites claiming to be a people of God but not really believing that God can speak and we can hear?

There is a profound connection between experiencing God's unconditional love for us as imperfect, missing-the-mark individuals, and our ability to love others in the meeting who we clearly see are also imperfect and missing-the-mark. But that kind of love is exactly what God requires of us, what we claim as we call ourselves Friends. Thank God that we do not need to struggle in our own will power and strength to achieve this love. All we need to do is remain still and quiet and experience God's love for us. Then, when we are filled to overflowing, we will have ample to give to others. It will flow effortlessly and naturally. So let us turn to the task of helping each other risk being open to God's transforming love which sees into our darkest, secret corners with loving Light.

From Monthly Meeting minutes, 3/28/1993:
2. The Clerk read the following letter from Lynn Clark and Nancy Reeves; Ruth Brutz read the following response from Ministry and Oversight Committee. Shared heartfelt feelings followed. William Beasley's and Tom Cooke's names were added to the committee suggested by Ministry and Oversight. The Meeting approved this committee. We affirm our faith that God can reveal God's will to us and our faith that God will forgive us if we fail to follow God's word.

7. We recommend that the Committee on Ministry and Oversight be asked to state its willingness and availability to speak with and listen to, in a non-judgmental way, individuals who may feel the need of support and clearness.

Lois Edgerton, Clerk
Betty B. Lake, assistant clerk

Letter from Nancy Reeves and Lynn Clark, 3/7/1993
Dear Friends,

After much prayer and deliberation, we, Nancy Reeves and Lynn Clark, are led to ask you to take the first step toward taking our marriage and family under your care.

During the past six years, while the meeting struggled with the "policy" question of whether same gender marriages can be taken under the care of Cleveland meeting, we have felt increasingly isolated from the meeting. We experience, and are deeply grateful for, the care of many individuals for our marriage and family. It has, however, been quite painful to watch the corporate meeting find ways to move forward on other difficult issues while allowing one which personally affects our lives to sit on the back burner.

The past several months have been particularly stressful for our family. It is during these times, when we most need the support of our faith community, that we feel most keenly the lack of its support as a body. We hope that in changing the nature of our request, from a policy question to one of support and care for our individual family, way will open to proceed.

We ask that the Cleveland Meeting appoint a Clearness Committee to meet with us and explore whether, as we believe, our relationship is a marriage and whether or how it might be appropriate for the meeting to take our relationship and family under its care.

As with any request for clearness for marriage we are not asking the Meeting, at this time, to approve taking our marriage under its care. We are asking for it to appoint a committee to help discern our and the meeting's clearness to have our marriage taken under its care. We expect that such a committee would report back to the meeting as a whole, and any decision about whether or how to proceed on the basis of committee recommendations would be made by the meeting at that time.

Report from Ministry and Oversight Committee to Monthly Meeting, 3/28/1993

Nancy and Lynn believe that they are married to each other and are asking the meeting for a clearness committee to help them discern whether or not they are correctly naming their relationship. This clearness committee would also explore with them how the meeting and Lynn and Nancy and [their daughter] Emma could be mutually supportive of each other. We suggest for this committee: Marty Grundy, Conleth Crotser, David Male, and Joyce Callahan.

Ruth Brutz, Clerk of Ministry and Oversight Committee

From Monthly Meeting minutes, 4/25/1993:

7. Connie Bimber gave the Lake Erie Yearly Meeting's report. "In the Manner of Friends" is the theme for this year's annual meeting to be held at Bluffton College, Sixth Month 17-20, 1993. LEYM has asked us to consider the following minute:

LEYM Minute on Diversity

As Quakers we recognize "that of God in everyone," the sacredness of every person as part of the divine creation. We believe that cultivating a deeper awareness of our relatedness to all persons, everywhere, enables us to live more Spirit-filled and thus more joyous lives.

So, in keeping with "the Spirit of Christ, by which we are guided," we seek to recognize and include, as our brothers and sisters, the community of gays and lesbians who suffer from exclusion and rejection by many in our society and who are increasingly subject to derision and violence. We seek always to heal the separation caused by intolerance; to recognize the diversity of humanity; and to live in an ever more loving and peaceful association with our fellow human beings.

10. The Clerk read two letters, one from Evelyn Culver and one from William Shea [resigning from all committees]. We pray that God's will be made clear to us on this matter.

Lois Edgerton, Clerk
Betty B. Lake, Assistant Clerk

Letter to Cleveland Friends Meeting, 4/25/1993

It makes me very sad to see members of our Meeting feel hostility towards those who do not agree that there should be an acceptance of same sex marriage and who believe that God speaks to them in confirmation of what they personally want to believe.

The unwillingness to accept the idea that all Quakers in the Meeting may not come to an agreement over same sex marriage and to continue to pressure others - makes me very sad.

Setting up a Clearness Committee, such as I understand has been done, may give the impression that there is more of a consensus or agreement, and that this added pressure may result in an agreement, but I am concerned that it may cause more conflict and less Insight.

I do appreciate and approve of a committed relationship between individuals, but I still maintain a marriage is and should be a relationship between a man and a woman.

I am not sure God is speaking through me - I do not understand why other people are so sure God speaks through them, urging or approving of same sex marriage.

If God is love, there seems to me to be no reason why we cannot strive to love each other even though we disagree.

E.J.C.

From the *Tatler*, Second through Fifth Month 1993
News and Community Notes

Nancy Reeves was one of two FLGC representatives to attend the general Board of the National Council of Churches last November here in Cleveland. Along with representatives from other gay and lesbian church groups they were sharing concerns among the various groups struggling for equality within their denominations, and were supporting the request of the Universal Fellowship of Metropolitan Community Church for observer status at the NCC. This was denied by a vote of 90-81.

Got a postcard from Carolyn Rudd: "We do hope Cleveland meeting can see clearness to bring open hearts and souls into God's love and become channels, indeed examples, for carrying and reflecting that love to all God's creatures, while not judging them."

Letter from Ministry and Oversight Committee to Salem Quarterly Meeting for Ministry and Oversight, 4/29/1993

Two women, one a member and the other an active attender of our meeting, have come to us expressing their belief that they are married to each other and asking for our help in discerning if their belief is correct and exploring how our meeting could better relate to them as a couple and a family (they have a daughter, age 2). This is not an easy request, nor is it one which we take lightly. For years we have struggled to determine what for us is the loving Christian response to same-gender couples while these friends have struggled to find acceptance in our midst.

We feel that it is our duty as Friends to aid them in their discernment of God's leading, to love them regardless of the outcome of their search, and to consider their request for recognition and acceptance. Consequently we have appointed a committee of our members which is considering these matters.

We also feel it is especially important at this time to ask the ministers and overseers of Salem Quarterly Meeting for your prayers that our meeting, this committee, these two women and their child be guided by the infinite love and wisdom of our precious Lord, strengthened to heed God's commandments, forgiven if we stumble, and drawn ultimately into God's grace.

We realize that many in our Yearly Meeting have strong feelings about these matters, and some are deeply troubled that they are considered at all. Of those who feel hurt by our actions we ask forgiveness.

Wise parents know that they can advise, they can admonish, they can show by example, but ultimately the children become responsible for their own lives. So it is with each of us. While we appreciate and need your wisdom, your guidance, and your example, we accept our responsibility for discerning God's will.

For Cleveland Monthly Meeting for Ministry and Oversight,

Quentin Quereau, Clerk

From Monthly Meeting minutes, 6/27/1993

8. The report of the clearness committee for Nancy Reeves and Lynn Clark has been presented. We ask that it be printed in the *Tatler*. We appreciate the prayerful attention of the committee to its work. We have begun a discussion of the report, and hold it over to next month's Meeting for Business. We are reminded that the purpose of any Meeting for Business is to come into the pres-

ence of God. That is what the committee experienced, and its report is the result of the unity that committee members discovered in that Presence. We are urged to trust that God can bring our entire Meeting into God's unifying Presence.

Lois Edgerton, Clerk
Betty B. Lake, assistant clerk

Report of the Clearness Committee for Nancy Reeves and Lynn Clark, 6/3/93

"For the right joining in marriage is the work of the Lord only, and not the priests and magistrates; for it is God's ordinance and not man's; and therefore Friends cannot consent that they should join them together: for we marry none; it is the Lord's work, and we are but witnesses." (George Fox, 1669)

In the light of this understanding of the traditional Friends' position on marriage, we acknowledge that we do not have the authority to name the relationship of Nancy Reeves and Lynn Clark a marriage or not a marriage. We are satisfied that *they* believe that their relationship of unconditional love and commitment, emotional and family relationships, is by any definition which does not specify gender, a marriage; they feel there is no other word that fits as well. We are satisfied that they are being faithful to God's leadings as they experience them. The fruit of their obedience seems good to us: "love, joy, peace, patience, kindness, generosity, faithfulness, gentleness, and self-control. There is no law against such things." (Gal 5:22 NRSV)

We recognize that it is very difficult for many Friends to understand or accept the recognition that other than gender, marriage is the best term to describe Nancy's and Lynn's relationship. We recognize that there are passages in the Bible that condemn promiscuous and idolatrous homosexual acts; but we find nothing that addresses the question of committed, loving, monogamous same-gender relationships. Although their relationship seems to violate tradition and the common interpretation of scripture, we have found nothing compelling in God's law as written in the Old or New Testament that could prohibit its recognition or force its dissolution.

We have discovered that it is not our business to name this relationship. In our attempts over the years to do so we have failed to attend to our business of loving and supporting these friends. As we witness the relationship God creates between a couple by taking that couple's relationship under the care of the meeting, let us take the relationship between Nancy and Lynn under the care of Cleveland Friends Meeting. By that we mean to support this couple as they attempt to chart their course through the difficulties that life presents. This will probably require our celebrating and witnessing this relationship in a special called meeting in the manner of Friends.

We witness to the relationship between Nancy and Lynn and of their family. We acknowledge with high seriousness that we break precedent with the dominant culture of the western world, even as Friends on occasion have done before. We are humbled by our audacity. God is our judge. If Nancy and Lynn are wrong and their relationship is not a marriage, we are guilty of encouraging a wrong thing. We have faith that God sees our hearts and our earnest desire to follow Christ's command to love, and will forgive us if we have done wrong.

We find that Jesus summed up the law and prophets as flowing from the following: "The first is, 'Hear, O Israel: the Lord our God, the Lord is one; you shall love the Lord your God with all your heart, and with all your soul, and with all your mind, and with all your strength.' The second is this, you shall love your neighbor as yourself. There is no other commandment greater than these." (Mark 12:28-31, NRSV. See also Matt 22:36-40) Jesus also defined a Christian. He said, "This is my commandment, that you love one another as I have loved you. No one has greater love than this, to lay down one's life for one's friends. You are my friends if you do what I command you." (John 15:12-14. See also John 13:34, 14:15, 21, 23; 15:17.)

We have discovered that when the Meeting offers unconditional love it becomes easier for us to open ourselves to God's leadings and to have the courage to let go of our personal desires and idols and move into more faithful obedience to God. Our task as members of the Meeting is to learn how to love the way Jesus loved his disciples and asks us to love one another. We understand that this is not license. We direct each other to the law God has written on each of our hearts, trusting that in God's way and time we will be led into unity and wholeness. We ask the Meeting to take on this task of learning how to love God and love one another.

We recognize that witnessing to the love and commitment that we see breaks with common interpretation of tradition. As we accept Nancy, Lynn and Emma, we also accept our share of the burden of misunderstanding and persecution they may experience. If Cleveland Meeting accepts this witness, all of us then stand with Nancy, Lynn and Emma.

There is one other thing to which this committee can witness. That is the process we have experienced. In four meetings we dealt with the easy issues, then we laid our own hopes and expectations on the table and saw their divergence. We tasted despair that we humans could figure out a way forward. We then shifted from trying to produce a result to trying to come into the presence of God. Inexplicably and without the adrenaline rush of group dynamics or the mountaintop exhilaration of a mystical experience, we realized that we had come into unity. Our caveats, desires, and hesitations had just simply disappeared. We are grateful for God's gracious response to the many prayers asking for God's help and guidance and for the tendering of each of our hearts. It is hard to put into words because it is not a rational process; we witness to its reality.

 Marty Grundy, Conleth Crotser, David Male, and Joyce Callahan

Response to "Report of the Clearness Committee for Nancy Reeves and Lynn Clark" by W.D.S.

FIRST PARAGRAPH: For a while early Friends followed this statement and allowed anyone to come into their Meetings for Worship and marry themselves without oversight by the meeting. After a number of poor matches were made by couples not suited for each other, Friends backed off this statement and took on oversight of marriages. There is truth in this statement but it needs to be tempered because not all matches are God's Work.

Same sex matches are not God's work because they are contrary to Scripture (Genesis 2:24, Leviticus 18:22, Matthew 5:17, Romans 1:26-28). George Fox would have never agreed to them.

SECOND PARAGRAPH: We don't name the relationship because God has already named it as between man and woman (Genesis 2:24). We have no right to change God's word (Matthew 5:17-19). Continuing revelation was never meant to be contrary to former revelations in Scripture.

We do have a Scriptural right not to name this a marriage but not visa versa. We should not be satisfied that they are following God's Word when what they are doing is contrary to Scripture if their relationship is sexually consummated. Regardless of the above negatives, there is no positive Scriptural basis to marry them or witness their marriage. Marriage should be a positive testimony that God approves the relationship and not just us.

THIRD PARAGRAPH: "Promiscuous and idolatrous homosexual acts" which are an abomination to God (Leviticus 18:22) are a part of the sexual consummation of a homosexual marriage if we are to be gender neutral with respect to that Scriptural passage. (You must not lie with a man as with a woman: that is an abomination.) Marriage is to satisfy sexual as well as social needs (1 Corinthians 7:8-9).

Cleveland Meeting is a part of a Ohio Yearly Meeting which accepts the "traditional and common interpretation of marriage." The act of marrying Nancy and Lynn will cause either the disownment of Cleveland Meeting or the resignation of many yearly meeting members. This I have been told directly by those members. That plus the Scriptural reasons given above should be "compelling" enough reasons not to marry them.

FOURTH PARAGRAPH: If "it is not our business to name ... relationship(s)," any couple or group could claim marriage by us (uncles to nieces, children to parents etc.)

This "couple" receives a great deal of support in their friendship from the meeting without marriage.

FIFTH PARAGRAPH: God "will forgive" where there is repentance. Christ's commandment to love is not license to sin and love does not make a wrong become license to sin and Love does not make a wrong become right. Repentance forgives wrongs by Christ's death but even His death does not make wrong right. If we believe "God is our judge", we should read our Bibles and try to please God. God is more than a judge but a loving parent who sent his son and prophets and apostles to instruct us. Listen to them.

SIXTH PARAGRAPH: If we "loved God with all your heart" we would not perform this desolating sacrilege at our alter. God's ways are not. our ways. We are placing our love for Lynn and Nancy above our love for God which is wrong. Read Scripture and learn God's Ways.

SEVENTH PARAGRAPH: If "what God has written on each of our hearts" is not what God has written in the Book, we probably have been listening to the wrong God. It is not written on the hearts of those in Ohio Yearly Meeting. Why? Could it be their God is different?

We can love Nancy and Lynn without marrying them. They have testified that they have appreciated what they have experienced in Ohio Yearly Meeting and wish to remain a part of it - so they can apparently experience love without being married. The Love they experienced there was Jesus Christ. Perhaps the love Cleveland Meeting offers is incomplete because its source is different.

EIGHTH PARAGRAPH: Christians, not Lynn and Nancy, are persecuted, ostracized and discouraged in our meeting.

NINTH PARAGRAPH: Jesus Christ is not the only spiritual entity who can provide "mountaintop exhilaration." Having been in Hinduism, I can testify other spiritual entities provide such "mystical experiences." Many in our meeting worship light and do not know Christ. Satan himself masquerades as an angel of light so it is easy for his agents to masquerade as agents of good (2 Corinthians 11:14-15). I believe the committee has been deceived.

Quotations for the most part are from the committee's statement to provide reference to what I am referring to in each of the paragraphs.

From Monthly Meeting minutes, 7/23/1993

6. Marty Grundy suggested that we have some dialogue between the Clearness Committee for Lynn Clark and Nancy Reeves and Monthly Meeting members. This was approved and we started this process with prayerful meditation.

Lois Edgerton, Clerk
Betty B. Lake, assistant clerk

Letter from Salem Quarterly Meeting for Ministry and Oversight, 7/31/1993

Dear Quentin Quereau,

It was good to talk to thee over the phone. The Quarterly Meeting M & O always feels so pressed for time. With that attitude it is difficult to wait on a full understanding. There seemed to be some confusion about whether the complete minute or only part of it was to be shared with your M & O. I guess I will send it on to thee and thee may perhaps want to discuss it with David Male and Connie McPeak. It is all recorded as one minute, but I think David particularly felt the last paragraph sufficient to send to you.

Last Fifth Month Cleveland Monthly Meeting for Ministry and Oversight brought our attention to some matters that have deeply distressed us. Although their expressed purpose was to seek our prayers, as we pray we are often given understanding. The enclosed letters from Winona, Salem and Middleton Monthly Meetings for Ministry and Oversight unanimously express those meetings disunity with any recognition of a same gender marriage. As Friends of Jesus we do not condone sin in ourselves, nor in others. We encourage all to live in righteousness. The Bible as well as our Discipline state that marriage is a blessing of the Lord and reserved for a man and a woman. It has been recommended that this cause of discord, which separates Cleveland from the three other Monthly Meetings be settled quickly. We hope our disapproval is a loving warning that God's judgments cannot be changed to accommodate our own desires. As fellow members of Salem Quarterly Meeting, what each one does is the responsibility of the whole Quarterly Meeting. Although our spirits have greatly grieved in this consideration we are grateful to Cleveland for sharing this burden with us, because it has caused us to go to our Lord in a deeper way.

We appreciate that a Cleveland committee for clearness is convinced that they have been led by the Lord in their deliberations. We also feel that they should consider the concerns of the other three Monthly Meetings. We desire that everyone concerned feel our deep love and that hearts not be hardened. We seem to have two different directions of understanding and neither feels that the other is willing to listen or acknowledge as valid their direction. We all must continue to seek God's direction.

In Christian Love, Nancy A. Hawkins, Clerk

From Monthly Meeting minutes, 8/29/1993

11. We have considered again the Report of the Clearness Committee for Nancy Reeves and Lynn Clark, and the fuller explanation given last month of the Committee's experience. One Friend believes that the Committee, its process, and its report are spiritually defective and does not think we should proceed on it. Otherwise, Friends agree to receive the Report as an expression of the experience of the Committee, recognizing that not everyone in the meeting has unity with the recommendations in the Report. Some folks think we cannot take action without unanimity. Others understand that a minute reflects the sense of where the meeting is

at a given moment. We pray that we all surrender our personal agendas, open our hearts to God, and be guided by Christ's Spirit. We understand that the process of considering the meeting's response to the Clearness Committee's recommendations is held over until next month.

Lois Edgerton, Clerk
Marty Grundy, Recording Clerk for the day

From Monthly Meeting minutes, 9/26/1993

6. In reference to the report of the Clearness Committee for Nancy Reeves and Lynn Clark, the Clerk read a letter written by Esther Greenleaf Murer to the *Friends Journal* October 1993. We then followed the suggestion to have some time for meditation to pray about this issue—a time when Friends could express and share their feelings. There is to be a specially called Quarterly Meeting Ministry and Oversight Committee meeting Tenth Month 10, 1993 at 2:00 p.m. at the Salem Meeting House. It has been suggested and approved that time be spent each Monthly Meeting for Business in worship, waiting for God's will for us as a meeting to become known to us, in response to the Clearness Committee's recommendation.

Lois Edgerton, Clerk
Betty B. Lake, assistant clerk

From called meeting of Salem Quarter's Ministry & Oversight Committee, 10/10/93:

We are here to seek the will of God to resolve a difference of belief that has come between Cleveland Monthly Meeting and the three other Monthly Meetings of Salem Quarter.

Two women in the Cleveland Meeting desire that their relationship be recognized by the meeting as a marriage. Margaret Starbuck has read a letter she received from one of the women (Nancy Reeves) indicating her willingness to be open to the decision of Cleveland Meeting. They will not withdraw their request unless they feel led by God to do so.

It is suggested that if Cleveland Meeting does honor and recognize the couple as married in God's eyes they have chosen not to honor the Bible or our discipline. In this decision they would separate as a meeting from Salem Quarterly Meeting. Jesus does not condemn individuals, but he does call us each to repentance and holiness in our lives. We find no Biblical basis for a marriage between two men or two women. Our Ohio Yearly Meeting discipline is also clear that marriage is between a man and a woman.

Nancy A. Hawkins, Clerk

The above minute was never forwarded to Salem Quarterly Meeting, nor was it agreed upon more strongly than as a <u>suggestion</u>. In other words, there was not unity that this was to be recommended as definitive policy.

At this meeting the following letters from the other three monthly meeting ministry and oversight committees of Salem Quarter were circulated.

To Salem Quarterly Meeting for Ministry and Oversight [from Salem-Upper Springfield Monthly Meeting's M&O]:

We have seen the report from a Clearness Committee appointed by Cleveland Meeting on behalf of two women who seek to have their relationship recognized as a marriage. This report greatly disturbs us. Our clear understanding of the Scriptures and the Discipline is that these women and Cleveland Meeting are in jeopardy of dire consequences, and they must recognize that they will be called to account, first by the Lord and possibly by the Yearly Meeting. This body will also have to answer for the way in which we handled this situation.

Accepting this relationship is encouraging sin, and Friends should go on record as opposing sin. If we recognize this relationship as a marriage, what other situations are we going to be asked to tolerate?

The Bible as well as the Discipline state that marriage is a blessing of the Lord, and is reserved for a man and a woman, and to go against the dictates of the Lord will surely result in serious consequences.

Neither the people involved, nor the specific sin are the real issue, but as Christians, we must not condone sin. We are not trying to be judgmental either, for each one of us is burdened with sin. We MUST be more open to the healing and cleansing work of the Lord Jesus Christ.

We should not allow Satan to gain any foothold. If we unify against him, we will gain victory. We recognize that this situation is being used as a divisive tool of the enemy and we strongly recommend that it be settled quickly and not drag on any longer.

In Proverbs 6:16-19, Solomon lists the seven things the Lord hates and the seventh is, "one who sows discord among the brethren."

We, of Salem Upper-Springfield Monthly Meeting of Ministry and Oversight are united in the conviction that the recognition of this relationship as a marriage is wrong. We ask Cleveland Meeting to prayerfully and lovingly take action accordingly.

Ardith E Henderson	Carey L Newlin	Robert S Stratton
Alfred E Warrington	J Edward Henderson	Harry W Peacock Winifred E
Stratton	Lenna M Warrington	Archibald L Newlin Margaret
V Starbuck	Laura E Sturgeon	

To Salem Quarterly Meeting for Ministry and Oversight, 7-15-93 [from Middleton Monthly Meeting's M&O]

Middleton Friends Meeting for Ministry and Oversight believes that in God's eyes same sex relationships are wrong. We love your souls, but we cannot condone anything that is contrary to the teaching of Christ Jesus in your way of life. We believe that the scriptures are God inspired and that our discipline is a guideline to keep us in God's will.

Floyd H. Sidwell	Everett W. Hartley	Thomas C. Cooper
Elmer D. Cope	William L. Cope	Mary R. Hawkins
Mildred E. Cooper	Morris L. Kirk	Mary Eva Stanley
Virginia W. Cope	Nancy A. Hawkins	A. Marie Kirk

To Salem Quarterly Meeting for Ministry and Oversight, 5-27-1993 [from Winona Monthly Meeting's M&O]

We are saddened that Cleveland Meeting finds it necessary to even consider the question of recognizing same sex relationships as a marriage.

According to both the Bible and the Discipline of Ohio Yearly Meeting regarding marriage; this union is between a man and a woman.

We would recommend that anyone not abiding by our Discipline concerning marriage should be dealt with. We request that the Quarterly Meeting of Ministry and Oversight act on this recommendation before the 1993 Yearly Meeting.

The persons involved are not the issue—they may be kind, considerate, loving people; but an injustice is being done by not pointing them to the Saviour, Jesus Christ, who in His redemptive love will forgive the repentant sinners and save their souls from death.

We realize this is a permissive age and there is need for much repentance and prayer. We all have sinned and come short of the glory of God and must seek His forgiveness.

We will continue to pray that God's will may be done.

Winona Meeting for Ministry and Oversight:

Richard Hill	Margaret Hill	Evelyn Sidwell
Rebecca Ward	Richard Riley	Howard Bailey
Rose Sidwell	Myrtle Bailey	Esther Heacock

From Monthly Meeting minutes, 10/31/1993

5. Ministry and Oversight Committee reports that it has received a letter from Erma and William Shea resigning from Cleveland Meeting of the Religious Society of Friends. . . .

6. We have reread the letter of 3/7/93 from Nancy Reeves and Lynn Clark, the recommendation from Ministry and Oversight to name a clearness committee, the minute of 3/28/93 doing so, and the report of the clearness committee. The Meeting feels that the clearness committee did its job as requested and now the Meeting will seek God's teaching for us on what to do next. While opening ourselves to God's teaching today we have been blessed with good and searching ministry.

Lois Edgerton, Clerk
Marty Grundy, Recording Clerk for the day

From Monthly Meeting minutes, 11/28/1993

7. Also, approved by the Meeting was Ministry and Oversight's minute in further response to the report of the Clearness Committee. This minute has been accepted with one change:

> We do not have the authority within Ohio Yearly Meeting of the Religious Society of Friends to marry same gender couples, but we have the responsibility under God to witness to the positive, loving relationships in our midst and to support all of our members in their efforts to follow the leadings of God. Nancy and Lynn believe they are married under God. We believe Nancy and Lynn are sincere. We have faith that God will lead all of us into unity in the sunlight of His Truth as we follow the leadings of Christ.
>
> We are reminded that whenever we have among us a loving, committed relationship that invites God into it, our Meeting has cause to celebrate that commitment. We are grateful to be able to meet together to stand in the face of this issue, give it to God, and participate in this spiritual adventure of listening and obeying.

Lois Edgerton, Clerk
Betty B. Lake, Assistant Clerk

1994

From Monthly Meeting minutes, 1/30/1994

5. William and Erma Shea had asked to be removed from the membership. Quentin Quereau read a proposed minute from Ministry and Oversight which follows:

> It is with regret that we acknowledge the termination of membership by Erma and William Shea. Their contributions to the life of Cleveland Meeting over many years have been enormous—serving faithfully on many committees, acting as co-clerks of the Meeting for a time, personalizing our connections to Salem Quarter and Ohio Yearly Meeting, and quietly going about tasks too numerous to mention. We pray for them as they seek another spiritual community with which to worship.

We all miss them. We approve, with regret, their being released from our membership rolls.

6. Quentin then gave the mid-year report from Ministry and Oversight.

7. We turned our attention to the M & O minute from the November meeting. Recognizing our inability to find clearness in our own strength and will, we agree to pray for one another and ask for God's guidance.

Lois Edgerton, Clerk
Betty B. Lake, Assistant Clerk

Excerpts from Ministry and Oversight Committee's Mid-Year Report, 1/1994

The report of the Clearness Committee for Nancy Reeves and Lynn Clark and its reception by the Meeting and by Salem Quarter have occupied the Committee for many months. In this and in all matters we have tried to be open to God's leading. Discernment of God's will, rather than arrival at a good human decision remains our goal.

In accordance with the *Book of Discipline* of Ohio Yearly Meeting, the Committee sought to meet with Erma and William Shea concerning their termination of membership. At the Sheas' request this meeting did not take place.

Quentin Quereau, clerk of Ministry and Oversight Committee

From Monthly Meeting minutes, 2/27/1994:

8. The Clerk read the minute #7 from last month, regarding Ministry and Oversight Committee's minute. Heartfelt sharing and discussion followed. Praying for each other is leading us to a deepening sense of spiritual communion, as well as showing us places where we need work.

Lois Edgerton, Clerk
Betty B. Lake, assistant clerk

From Monthly Meeting minutes, 4/24/1994:

9. The Clerk read part of the letter written to the Meeting from Nancy Reeves and Lynn Clark to Monthly Meeting 3/28/1993, and the minute from Monthly Meeting of 11/93. Marty Grundy read a minute from Ministry and Oversight Committee concerning these matters. Much heartfelt sharing followed. The minute was approved as amended:

> Because of our inability to agree about how to deal with Nancy's and Lynn's relationship we have failed to provide them with the loving support they need from their faith community, support they need as they chart their course through the often difficult circumstances that life presents. They have asked us directly to consider how we might take their relationship under our care and we need to respond.
>
> We propose the establishment of a Committee of Care for the Relationship of Nancy and Lynn. We understand that we care for a relationship by supporting the centrality of God in it, and in the ongoing, unfolding, discovery of what that means in the lives of the individuals. We expect this Committee to report to Ministry and Oversight Committee so that M&O can help the Meeting understand how it can support Nancy and Lynn.
>
> The task before Cleveland Meeting is to address seriously what it means to love the Lord our God with all our heart and mind and soul and strength and our neighbor as ourself. We understand that it is only as we experience God's unconditional love for us that we are enabled to love others as selflessly and fully as possible. We must put God in the center of our lives rather than our own fear, pride, ego, or desire for control, but we can't really do that in our own strength of will power. There is a paradox here: we can't love others as selflessly as possible without surrendering to God's empowering love. God's love comes as a gift, through grace. While there is nothing we can do to make it hap-

pen, there are things we can do to put ourselves in the place where grace abounds. We can pay attention to the Seed or Light within us, giving thanks, praying, reading the Bible, and expecting to see Love at work within and around us. The work of each of us in Cleveland Meeting is to be attentive to Christ, the Inward Teacher, and encourage each other to do the same.

We thank Nancy and Lynn for their faithful presence, keeping open to us the opportunity to go deeper in our search for God's will. We have been tempted to short circuit the sometimes excruciatingly painful and laborious effort to get beyond our attempt to please everyone (which we cannot do) and instead learn to concentrate on listening to the Inward Teacher and on being faithful as best we can to the truth we have been taught so far.

We have nothing to fear from the diligent search for God's truth, and we will surely be led safely as we follow what we find.

We expect to continue to explore this issue and/or hold it in prayer each month, and we agree to continue praying for each other.

Tom Cooke asked that his disapproval be minuted, and also that he chooses to stand aside.

11. The following names have been brought forth by Ministry and Oversight Committee to serve on the Committee of Care for the Relationship of Nancy and Lynn: Connie McPeak, Tom Cooke, Jody Taslitz, and William Beasley, pending their acceptance. If any are not able to serve, we ask that Ministry and Oversight name others.

Lois Edgerton, Clerk
Betty B. Lake, Assistant Clerk

From Cleveland Meeting's Annual Meeting, 5/22/1994

1. The Clerk read her Annual Message.

7. The issue of Nancy Reeves and Lynn Clark's Committee Report was brought forth for consideration. After much heartfelt sharing and discussion we came into unity that we adopt, with joy, this report. The Committee is asked to reconvene to discern specific ways the Meeting can support Nancy's and Lynn's relationship and family."

Lois Edgerton, Clerk
Betty B. Lake, assistant clerk

Annual Message from the Clerk, 5/1994

My message came to me in the form of a prayer.

Dear God, Creator of Life, who loved us first that we might love, thank you for revealing your love through Jesus Christ who taught us how to seek a heaven on earth and that the kingdom is within and that the two most important things for us to do are to love you and to love each other as we love ourselves.

Forgive us our unfulfilled promises to trust you. Help us to understand our inward experiences so that our outward actions will reflect that experience. Help us to let go. Help us to let go of our need for absolutes and security, of our wish to be comfortable, of our wish to have all members and attenders to be in accord with our feelings, of our wish to be right and others wrong. As prejudices leave us, room is made in our hearts for you. Help us remember that Christ was persecuted for not fitting the people's interpretation of the doctrines of the Scriptures.

We are a community and in our worship feel a oneness that is shared. Help us to hold that experience of oneness as we open ourselves to each other to expose our differences. Help us to strip ourselves of outer influences so that we can become more centered. Help us to seek out that of God in each other—to accept and respect each other's paths before we proceed with any issue at hand. In other words, give our Meeting what it needs to be whole.

We ask all of this through the Spirit of Jesus Christ.
Amen.

Lois Edgerton, Clerk

From Monthly Meeting minutes, 6/26/94

4. The Clearness Committee for Nancy Reeves and Lynn Clark met as Annual Meeting had requested, and Conleth Crotser presented a report from the Committee. We still struggle with finding human words to clearly describe leadings from God. The Committee presented three recommendations. With a slight change in wording, the first recommendation was accepted: Meeting members have a special, called meeting for worship, on the 10th day of Ninth Month (Sept. 10) 1994, to celebrate and witness as Nancy and Lynn affirm what they know before God to be a marriage with one another. A celebration planning committee was named: William and Liz Beasley, Conleth Crotser, Peter Crowley, Joyce Callahan, and Ruth Brutz. The meeting approves the second recommendation and directs our clerk to write a letter to the court supporting Lynn's adoption of Emma. We also approve the meeting's reaffirmation of support for all couples and families within the meeting. Conrad Lindes disapproves but stands aside from the first two recommendations, and asks to be so recorded.

Lois Edgerton, Clerk
Debra Frantz, Recording Clerk

Clearness Committee for Nancy Reeves & Lynn Clark
Second Report as amended by monthly meeting, 6/26/1994

The original report from the Clearness Committee for Nancy Reeves and Lynn Clark was accepted by the Cleveland Friends' Meeting at the Fifth Month meeting for business. It was done in a process of coming into the presence of God, and achieving unity, that was very similar to what the Clearness Committee members had experienced, and that had enabled us to complete our original task.

Once this report was accepted, the same Committee was asked to reconvene. The Committee members were given the new task of discerning what specific steps Cleveland Friends Meeting members could follow to take under our care the relationship between Nancy and Lynn, and to care for their family, as well. The Committee recommends these three actions:

1. The Meeting members have a special, called meeting for worship, on the 10th day of Ninth Month (Sept. 10) 1994, to celebrate and witness as Nancy and Lynn affirm what they know before God to be a marriage with one another.

2. The Meeting send a letter, as requested by the court, in support of Lynn's efforts to adopt Emma.

3. The Meeting members take this time to reaffirm our support for this couple and family, and all couples and families in the meeting, as their relationships develop, through both good times and struggles. We understand that we care for a relationship by supporting the centrality of God in it, and in the ongoing, unfolding, discovery of what that means in the lives of the individuals.

> Committee members Nancy Reeves, David Male, Marty Grundy,
> Conleth Crotser, Tom Cook, Lynn Clark, Joyce Callahan,
> and William Beasley

Excerpt from Report on North Carolina Yearly Meeting (Conservative), 7/13-17/1994:

Connie McPeak and Marty Grundy visited this sister yearly meeting at their annual sessions held at Chowan College, Murfreesboro, NC, 7/13-17, ...

Durham Meeting reported that after a lengthy process it has come to clearness that it should offer the same marriage procedure to same gender couples as to heterosexual ones. Two visitors from Ohio YM(C) reacted strongly, and questioned what this meant for the *Book of Discipline.* Then several older and weighty Friends rose to express their own lack of comfort with same gender marriage, but their faith in the process through which the decision was reached. They spoke of the Light shown on each of our paths, and trusting it. The yearly meeting felt no need to rush to action, recognizing that several other meetings were also dealing with the issue.

NCYM(C) truly functions as a place in which individual Friends and meetings can come to test their leadings, to gain from the wisdom and experience of others, and to grow in faith and love. The worship was deep. Love and caring were palpable. That does not mean there were no problems. . . . We came away renewed and refreshed.

> Marty Grundy

Friends in Cleveland Meeting who were unhappy sought sympathetic ears in OYM, and some OYM Friends spoke to CFM folks.

From the *Tatler*, 7/1994:
Help Needed
Volunteers are needed for Nancy Reeves' and Lynn Clark's celebration on Saturday, Sept. 10. Please contact Ruth Brutz at 663-2571 if you can help with any of the following: housing for out-of-town guests, setting up Sat. morning, 8 a.m.; card tables and/or folding chairs; greeters; childcare; food (salads or desserts).

Joyce Callahan

From Monthly Meeting minutes, 7/31/94
4. Marty Grundy reported from the Clearness Committee for Nancy Reeves and Lynn Clark. The Committee proposed the following revision to the minute presented at Sixth Month meeting for business. The Meeting approved the minute as presented:

> We reaffirm the experience of our initial minute (6/93), that God has led us to understand it is not our business to name this relationship a marriage or not a marriage. Furthermore, we reaffirm that we acknowledge Nancy's and Lynn's belief that God has joined them in marriage. We understand they will make anew their covenant with one another in a special called meeting for worship as the Cleveland Monthly Meeting of the Religious Society of Friends takes their relationship and family under its care.

Lois Edgerton, Clerk
Debra H. Frantz, Recording Clerk

A short announcement in the 8/1994 Tatler *did not use the same careful wording that the clearness committee and monthly meeting had come to understand was critically important. We thought the wording was inspired because by refusing to name the relationship as "marriage", leaving that to God, it could have enabled us to continue in fellowship with Ohio Yearly Meeting. However, the wording used in the* Tatler *was read by Friends in Ohio Yearly Meeting, serving to confirm their suspicion that we really were approving same sex marriage in direct defiance of the OYM(C)* Book of Discipline.

From the *Tatler*, 8/1994:
Nancy Reeves and Lynn Clark Celebration
Lots of volunteers are needed and welcome to help with preparations for the September 10 celebration of the marriage of Lynn Clark and Nancy Reeves. Anyone interested in volunteering for the following tasks should contact Ruth Brutz at 663-2571.
1. Overnight accommodations (either 9/9 or 9/10 or both nights).
2. Saturday morning (9/10) setup for meeting and reception.
3. Saturday afternoon cleanup, return rented tent, etc.
4. Make a salad or dessert for the reception!
5. Childcare on Saturday 9/10 from 1:00 to 4:00 p.m.

Letter from the Clerk of Salem Quarterly Meeting's Ministry and Oversight Committee to the Clerk of Cleveland Meeting's Ministry and Oversight Committee, 9/17/1994:
The letter began by quoting the minute of 10/10/1993, see page 44 above.

The above minutes were taken almost eleven months ago, at a meeting in which many of the Cleveland Ministry and Oversight members were present. We need to consider the recent actions of Cleveland Monthly Meeting. A minute of recommendation needs to be sent from Salem Quarterly Meeting for Ministry and Oversight to the Salem Quarterly Meeting for Business. The hour before the regular Quarterly meeting business meeting seems a little short to work this out (if only because we tend to be uneasy when the meeting runs into the next time slot). Please speak with thy Ministry and Oversight members and get back to me with their recommendation.

Nancy A. Hawkins, clerk

Letter from Cleveland Meeting's Ministry and Oversight Committee to the Clerk of Salem Quarterly Meeting's Ministry and Oversight Committee, 9/30/1994

Dear Nancy,

Cleveland Meeting's Ministry and Oversight Committee met September 29. We wish to invite all of Salem Quarterly Meeting's Ministry and Oversight Committee to meet in Cleveland either Sunday, October 23, or Sunday, November 6, at 2:00 p.m. We invite as many as can do so to worship with us at 11:00 a.m. whichever Sunday the Meeting for Ministry and Oversight is to take place.

In order that Cleveland Meeting's response to the relationship of Nancy Reeves and Lynn Clark may be clear, we summarize as follows:

At our Annual Meeting 5/22/94 Friends were brought into unity, sensing that God has instructed us to accept the 6/27/93 report of the Clearness Committee for Nancy Reeves and Lynn Clark (which is enclosed) and thus calls us to witness to Nancy's and Lynn's relationship and family.

We remain faithful to our leading that we do not have the authority to name the relationship of Nancy Reeves and Lynn Clark a marriage or not a marriage. We are satisfied that they are being faithful to God's leadings as they experience them. In witnessing to their relationship, which has been growing for 13 years, we are being faithful to God's leadings as we experience them.

Many times throughout history Christians have been called upon to reach out to God's forgotten children, be they Samaritans, Gentiles, slaves, drunks, thieves, or children of unwed mothers and their parents. This is often done at great personal risk and with great personal hardship. As God loves, accepts and forgives us, we try to love, accept and forgive each other, including our gay and lesbian F/friends.

We look forward to hearing from you regarding the date for meeting (October 23 or November 6).

On behalf of Cleveland Meeting for Ministry and Oversight,

Quentin Q. Quereau, Clerk

From Monthly Meeting minutes, 10/30/1994:

9. Friends reminded us that Ministry and Oversight Committee will need our prayers this week as they prepare spiritually for the called Quarterly Meeting of Ministry and Oversight next Sunday. Friends also will pray for Nancy Hawkins, Clerk of Quarterly Meeting for Ministry and Oversight, and for all those who will be attending the Quarterly Meeting.

Lois Edgerton, Clerk
Debra Frantz, Recording Clerk

Sunday afternoon, **11/6/94 Salem Quarterly Meeting for Ministry and Oversight** *had a special called meeting, lasting a bit over 3 hours. After the clerk read the opening minute, and letters from the M & O of Middleton (of which she is clerk) and of Winona, there was a long silence, and then the sense of the meeting began to slowly reverse. A Friend spoke against separation, and another said he was not in unity with his meeting's letter. Another Friend later, at the end, expressed to us his uneasiness with it, as well.*

This is the minute extract which was forwarded to the Quarterly Meeting. This is also only as much as was given to Cleveland Friends. The full minutes are a bit longer in the beginning, with a long Bible quotation, and perhaps some other material.

This meeting has been called because of our deep distress with Cleveland Meeting's affirmation and acknowledgment of two women's belief that God has joined them in marriage and of their holding a special meeting for worship to witness and support their covenant with one another.

Minutes have been received from Winona and Middleton preparative meetings for ministry and oversight clearly stating the above named actions of Cleveland Meeting to be contrary to their sense of God's truth and in direct disobedience to the Holy Bible and our Discipline. We feel great sadness at the idea of a possible separation although some see this as already accomplished. Others have expressed a wish for another way.

We have been aware of this issue eight years and although we feel love for one another, we have not found unity on this issue. We hope in this next week all of us will be diligent in prayer that we each give up our own beliefs to know the wisdom of God for His unity. This minute will be forwarded to the next business meeting.

Nancy A. Hawkins, clerk

> *Three times Friends asked for an extra sentence to be added at the end to the effect that we experience (or have experienced) unity in God through Jesus Christ; twice a sentence was offered about having sufficient faith that God will bring us into unity if we let go of our own desire to control the outcome. But the clerk seemed unable to write these into the minutes. She did make a number of minor changes that Friends requested.*
>
> Marty Grundy's notes, 11/1994

Minutes of Salem Quarterly Meeting, 11/12/94, in their entirety:
At our Quarterly Meeting held at Salem, Ohio, Eleventh Month 12, 1994

"Let us therefore no longer pass judgment on one another, but resolve instead never to put a stumbling block or hindrance in the way of another." (Romans 14:13 NRSV)

We have heard the reports from the monthly meetings, and all of the representatives named are present except one who has to work this morning and another who is unable to attend. We welcome Ken and Kathryn Jacobson, who will be Head of School and Director of Development at Olney Friends School soon.

We have heard the First and Second General Queries and the responses prepared by the Monthly Meetings. The following summaries have been approved as read and will be forwarded to the Yearly Meeting clerk.

SUMMARY OF RESPONSES TO THE FIRST GENERAL QUERY:

> One meeting reports that it could do better on punctuality, the other three are more punctual. We all hold our meetings in expectant waiting worship. Although our gospel ministry is not paid for with money, the reward of speaking faithfully is very great. We are paying attention to discerning when a message is for oneself and when it is to be shared with the whole group. As we learn to do more personal prayer and inner work at home we are freed to pray for the meeting and do corporate work during First Day worship.
>
> One meeting reports that it almost always has visitors. Friends are learning to be led by the Spirit in responses to individual visitors. We know that God is at work among us and we are finding ways to invite others to share in the hard work and rich blessings. As we welcome the presence of the Lord and the power of the Holy Spirit in our midst, we will have that special blessing that will excite us and make us eager to invite others into this experience.

SUMMARY OF RESPONSES TO THE SECOND GENERAL QUERY

> One meeting reports that because it is small Friends consider each other as family and therefore forgiveness comes easily. We acknowledge that it is difficult to love others as ourselves, and to love others as much as we love our family. One meeting acknowledges that they are not always careful in their speech for the reputations of others. Another

meeting notes that the rough times test and strengthen us; our spiritual life deepens as we experience our own limitations and turn to the Lord.

One meeting notes there are no major differences to disrupt them, although they are aware of situations in the past that have affected them. One meeting feels that we are held accountable for each others' spiritual lives. Another reminds us that if we walk in the path God directs us to, then any differences can be resolved in Christ. The differences in the wider fellowship of Friends make us sad, and we strive to seek Christ's Spirit in understanding and finding solutions to the problems within the Quarterly Meeting. The small differences seem insignificant when we seek the larger goal of life in Christ.

Martha Hartley received the collection for Monte Verde Friends School and the Olney Hostess Fund this year. We are informed that $209 has been collected for Monte Verde: $50 from Cleveland, $78 from Middleton, $71 from Salem, and $10 from Winona. There is $297 for the Olney Hostess Fund: $50 from Cleveland, $110 from Middleton, $87 from Salem, and $50 from Winona.

We have heard the minutes from our last Quarterly Meeting.

We have heard from Friends who attended the Yearly Meeting sessions in Eighth Month that we are always blessed with so much spiritual food. At the meeting for healing most testimony regarded spiritual rather than physical healing. The victory of Christ can not be defeated. Some of our traditions can be so strong they block new growth and new visions. Most business went smoothly, although one epistle required revisions and another was sent back to be rewritten. Becky Hawkins and Mary Alice Pino did a splendid job with the children. Floyd Sidwell spoke with them one day about what meeting was like when he was young. Myrtle Bailey worked with the young Friends on biographies of various Quakers, and the youth created a play about the prodigal son. The worship sharing in the mornings was particularly rich and helpful. Rejoice! We are invited to a great banquet! Go forth and share! But after we come home, there is a danger that maintaining our familiar situations takes precedence.

We have heard a minute from the Quarterly Meeting of Ministry and Oversight that some Friends are distressed by Cleveland Meeting's action in Ninth Month regarding two lesbian women, but there is no unity on what should be done.

With the exception of the representatives from Cleveland Meeting, most but not all Friends present feel that Cleveland Meeting by its action has disassociated itself from Salem Quarterly Meeting and Ohio Yearly Meeting. The Discipline does not say how a monthly meeting is to be disowned but we recognize that this is what has happened today, even though there is not unity on this course of action. Friends would like Cleveland Meeting to know that it can be reinstated if they change their behavior. We direct the Clerk to send a copy of this minute to Representative Meeting.

Friends agreed not to appoint at this time a nominating committee to bring forth names of Friends to replace members of Cleveland Meeting currently serving the Quarterly Meeting. Rather, Friends ask the Alternate Clerk to serve in place of the current Clerk at the next meeting.

The meeting concludes with announcements.

Martha J. P. Grundy, Clerk
E. Marlene Cooper, Assistant Clerk

From Middleton Monthly Meeting minutes, 11/23/1994

. . . An interesting account of Eleventh Month Quarterly meeting has been given by the representatives. It saddens us that Salem Quarterly Meeting's firm stand on upholding standards for marriage, as taught in the Holy Scriptures and outlined in our Book of Discipline, has resulted in the separation of Cleveland Monthly Meeting from membership with us. We shall miss them in our meeting fellowship, and pray that the Lord will bring good out of this situation, and heal the wounds of all concerned.

. . . We have been told that at the recent meeting of Representative Meeting it was decided that the remaining 3/4 of Cleveland's share of the apportionment will be divided among most of the remaining meetings of the yearly meeting. We are to be notified of our additional apportionment, by the yearly meeting treasurer.

Marie Kirk, Marlene Cooper, Clerks

From Monthly Meeting minutes, 11/28/1994:

5. Marty and Lois reported on the meetings of Salem Quarterly M & O and Salem Quarterly Meeting. Friends shared feelings and concerns, but clearness on how to proceed was not found and Friends determined to wait.

7. Friends decided not to consider whether we will continue to address Ohio YM's Queries, but hold this question for next month.

Lois Edgerton, Clerk
Debra Frantz, Recording Clerk

From Ohio Yearly Meeting Representative Meeting, 11/1994:

After discussion the following minute was prepared:

We have read a minute from a called meeting of the Salem Quarterly Meeting on Ministry and Oversight acknowledging that some Friends are distressed by Cleveland Meeting's action in Ninth Month, at which time they had a called meeting to witness and celebrate what two women are claiming to be a marriage to each other.

An excerpt from the minutes of Salem Quarterly Meeting held 11-12-1994 states that most, but not all, Friends present feel that Cleveland Meeting by this action has disassociated itself from Salem Quarterly Meeting and Ohio Yearly Meeting.

Same sex marriages are incompatible with our Discipline and our understanding of Biblical standards.

We are distressed by this action for deep friendships have been formed with members of Cleveland meeting. We hope that there may be those in Cleveland meeting who still wish to fellowship with us. They would be very welcome. It is our hope we all will seek to know the way to eternal life in Christ Jesus our Lord. We affirm our need to continue to pray for each other. May the Holy Spirit lead us all in the paths of truth and righteousness.

As of 11-12-1994 we shall consider Cleveland Monthly Meeting released from membership with Ohio Yearly Meeting. A copy of this minute will be sent to the clerk of Cleveland Monthly Meeting.

10. Cleveland Monthly Meeting has informed us they will pay one-fourth of their apportionment, since that is the approximate time which has elapsed since Yearly Meeting. The balance of their apportionment $2321.00 will be spread across the Yearly Meeting. Leonard Guindon, treasurer, will probably need help in figuring the new apportionments. Wilson Morlan and Paul Livezey have volunteered to help with this—we approve.

11. Our Nominating Committee will endeavor to appoint another member to the Walton Home Board to replace Constance McPeak. . . .

Myrtle Bailey, Clerk
Rose Sidwell, Assistant Clerk

From Monthly Meeting minutes, 12/18/1994:

8. We are reminded that this meeting has not minuted receiving from Rochester Monthly Meeting a report of the celebration of commitment held under its care in Sixth Month 1993 of Pamela Heggie and Nancy Newman, who were valued participants in our meeting community while they attended medical school here. Pam joined Friends through Cleveland Meeting and is still a member here. We acknowledge with joy their commitment to each other.

12. Conrad Lindes requested that Cleveland Meeting see how he might have dual membership with Winona Meeting because he feels he was deprived of membership in Salem Quarterly Meeting against his will. We ask Ministry and Oversight Committee to consider how this might be done.

Lois Edgerton, Clerk
Marty Grundy, Recording Clerk for the day

Letter from a member of Cleveland Meeting to the Assistant Clerk of Salem Quarterly Meeting, 12/21/1994;
Dear Ardith Henderson;

I write to you not as a committee member, but rather, about a special concern of mine. I would like to begin this communication by telling you a little about myself. I have lived in Cleveland with my husband and five children since moving from South America in 1948. I attended Earlham College for four years and graduated from the University of Wisconsin. My parents and grandparents were long time Quakers. I am 86 years old. My husband, a professor at CWRU, died two years ago. We were married for sixty years. My five children and nine grandchildren are scattered coast to coast. I transferred membership to the Cleveland Friends Meeting from the Spiceland Indiana Friends Church and have attended the Cleveland Meeting throughout the last forty years.

As a Meeting, we have struggled over many issues - the recent issue concerning a same-sex marriage has been intense for almost eight years. Most of the Meeting thought that even though we could not go forward with an actual legal marriage, there should be a religious service to recognize the loving relationship between these two individuals. Most of the Meeting felt God led them to this decision.

I have steadfastly felt we should love and care for these individuals, try to understand and seek guidance on their behalf. I did't feel then, and I don't feel now, that a person should withdraw from Quaker Meetings or be excluded from Quaker Meetings because he/she is not in total agreement. When I learned the Ohio Yearly Meeting was considering casting out the Cleveland Friends Meeting I was deeply saddened. This is my reason for writing to you.

The Cleveland Meeting has struggled and prayed for many years over the issue of same-sex marriage. While I am one of the few who did not feel led to take this position, still, I recognize why most of the Meeting felt called to sanction the relationship.

Forgive me for writing in this manner, but I feel one of the concepts of the Society of Friends is to seek the Truth, which we have done and continue to do. I believe differences of opinion are not reason enough to leave the Ohio Yearly Meeting or for us to be excluded from the Meeting. This is not the way we should treat each other. The Cleveland Meeting is trying to be faithful and to do what each believes is right. An honest dialogue might help all of us understand your spiritual basis for deciding that the Cleveland Friends Meeting is not worthy to continue a relationship with the Ohio Yearly Meeting, as a couple of the Quarterly Meetings have done. How, in your opinion, does God view this decision?

I urge the Ohio Yearly Meeting to be patient with the Cleveland Friends Meeting, helping us as we seek the truth and God's will. So many are carrying heavy burdens and we need your wisdom, your insight, your caring. The Ohio Yearly Meeting has been such an inspiration to the Cleveland Friends Meeting, it should not turn us away even though there has been a difference in interpreting God's will for our Meeting. Let us grow in our diversity and hope that love will strengthen all our relationships. Thank you for listening and caring.

Sincerely yours,

E. J. C.

Copy to Susan Smith [Clerk of Ohio Yearly Meeting]

Excerpt of a letter from a member of Salem-Upper Springfield Monthly Meeting to a member of Cleveland Meeting, 12/22/1994:

Dear Marty,

I very much appreciate receiving the *Tatler*, and I especially am grateful for thy article on the "Disownment." The term used by our Representative Meeting is "Disassociation." Don't know which is better or worse. Thee deals very well with the several issues involved. G. H. was dumbfounded at Quarterly Meeting. The matter had not been spoken of as a concern outside of our M&O and she, as I, is not in the groups that have discussed it at length. Evidently Middleton [Meeting] has had several meetings to discuss it. Next day, after Q[uarterly] Mtg., G. spoke in mtg. for worship—very plainly, saying we should be ashamed of ourselves for our narrowmindedness. She and E. have worshipped with Friends all over the world, & she said the hallmark of Friends was loving compassion. She couldn't believe what had happened. Then she walked out & went home! I was afraid she might withdraw her membership, but she was back that very afternoon helping with an open house—we were part of an Historic Church Tour. Sixty-one visitors came. G. has been attending & participating.

I feel a heaviness whenever I think of it! . . .

Our loving, warm greetings to all the Friends of the Cleveland Mtg. Love to thee, Marty,

M. S. and M. A.

1995

From Monthly Meeting minutes, 2/26/1995:

7. Quentin Quereau gave Ministry and Oversight Committee's report on the activities of the Committee since annual meeting last Fifth Month. The full report will be printed in the *Tatler*.

11. Conrad Lindes shared from his continuing correspondence with Friends in Salem Quarterly Meeting. It seems to be the perception of Friends in Salem Quarter that Cleveland Friends Meeting chose to leave. They do not feel we were disowned. Conrad requested that Cleveland send a letter to Salem Quarter stating that he was not a part of the decisions that led to the separation between Cleveland Meeting and Salem Quarter so that Winona Meeting may feel free to accept his membership. Conrad clarified that his intent is to be a full member in both meetings. Lois stated that she had no objection to writing a letter with the purpose of stating the truth about Conrad's concerns. Friends shared their continuing struggles with the issues surrounding the separation between Cleveland Friends Meeting and Salem Quarterly Meeting. Friends shared their convictions that the unity we reached last Fifth Month was at God's direction, not our own, but shared sorrow that the actions led to individual's feelings of alienation. Friends who were present at Salem Quarterly Meeting

last Eleventh Month stated that it was very clear at the time that we were being disowned. Friends also expressed the hopes that God would show us new opportunities to pursue a relationship with Friends in Salem Quarter. The meeting decided to turn Conrad's request over to Ministry and Oversight Committee for further consideration before deciding to write the requested letter.

Lois Edgerton, Clerk
Debra Haines Frantz, Recording Clerk

Excerpt from the Mid-winter Report of the Committee for Ministry and Oversight, 1/1995

Since making its Annual Report in May 1994, the Committee for Ministry & Oversight has worked in several areas, meeting once or twice each month as needed. Through the summer and fall a great deal of attention was given to our relationship to Salem Quarter. Since our disownment by the Quarter in November that relationship is still very much on our minds and hearts but no longer has the feeling of urgent attention it had before. We must be patient and remain open to whatever the future holds here. . . .

Quentin Quereau, clerk of Ministry and Oversight Committee

From Monthly Meeting minutes, 4/30/1995:

4. William Beasley brought a concern about the defining of our suspension of relationship with Ohio YM. Marty gave an update regarding the language that Ohio YM is using to explain what happened. It seems clear that although the minutes of the Eleventh Month Quarterly Meeting clearly state we were disowned, the minutes at Eleventh Month Representative Meeting state that we chose to disassociate and they released us—which is not true. Friends suggested we restate for the benefit of all involved the truth of what we experienced and our openness to continuing to work toward unity. Marty suggested that we draft a letter for consideration at Annual Meeting and that we can decide at that time to whom the letter should go. Marty Grundy, William Beasley, and Ruth Brutz will draft the letter.

Lois Edgerton, Clerk
Debra Haines Frantz, Recording Clerk

The lead article in the Spring 1995 Friends for Lesbian and Gay Concerns newsletter was about the disownment of Cleveland Friends Meeting.

Excerpt from a personal letter from a member of Stillwater Monthly Meeting 5/10/1995

Dear Marty,
   . . . I was at the Representative Meeting where the minute that disturbed thee was approved. In the meeting, what had happened at QM was described accurately as far as I could tell, and there was no doubt that the action had been taken at the QM's initiative not

Cleveland's. My belief is that the term "released" was used in an effort to be gentle, not to give the impression that Cleveland asked to leave.

There does seem to have been some misunderstanding as a result of the minute, though. Chesterfield Meeting members were under the impression that Cl. asked to leave until I convinced them otherwise. At next Rep. Meeting I hope to propose that an account of what happened, with minute extracts, be sent to all our monthly meetings to clear up any confusion about this.

Thee might be interested to know that New England YM's discipline spells out a procedure for discontinuing a meeting for disciplinary reasons. The QM has to approve the action for 3 consecutive years before it's final!

J. B.

Letter to Cleveland Meeting, 5/13/1995:
Dear friends,

We were grieved to learn in the Spring issue of the FLGC newsletter that your meeting was disowned by the Ohio Yearly Meeting for recognizing the relationship of a lesbian couple, Lynn Clark and Nancy Reeves.

We want to express our support for your meeting. We applaud your courage in following the Light as you understand it and sincerely hope that healing will be given to all who have been hurt in this painful struggle.

Pam Hughes, of behalf of the Lesbian & Gay Concerns Committee,
St. Louis Monthly Meeting

From Monthly and Annual Meeting minutes, 6/4/1995:

Ministry and Oversight Committee's Message. Quentin Quereau delivered the year's summary from the Ministry and Oversight Committee to the Meeting. [see below]

Prayer for one another. The meeting paused to spend a few minutes in prayer for one another.

OYM Letter. The Clerk read the portion of the minutes from last month calling for a letter to OYM clarifying the exact nature and circumstances of our disownment or release from OYM. The draft prepared by Ruth Brutz, William Beasley, and Marty Grundy was read aloud by Liz Beasley and copies were distributed to all present. Minor editing was done and the letter was approved pending final date and spelling checks. It was approved that the letter be sent to members of each Ministry and Oversight committee in OYM and all representatives. It will also be printed in the *Tatler*.

Lois Edgerton, Clerk
Respectfully submitted, William Beasley
(substituting for Debra Frantz)

Excerpt from the Annual Report from Ministry and Oversight Committee, 1995

The past year has been a very eventful one for Cleveland Friends Meeting. Eventful times have their own special character which can alternately sharpen or obscure our ability to be attentive to the Inner Guide. We have done our best to be attentive.

A year ago the meeting reached clarity in the ways we were to witness to the loving relationship between Nancy Reeves and Lynn Clark and to take their family under the care of the meeting. In September we celebrated their relationship and family with great joy in a called meeting for worship. In our witness and our care we are being faithful to God's leadings as we experience them.

In November, as a result of our witness, Cleveland Meeting was disowned by Salem Quarter. Individually and corporately we experienced sadness, pain, anger, and other emotions and continue to experience them in changing ways in the months since then. We are trying to find a patient path of love through these conflicting feelings: love for one another and love for members of Salem Quarter and Ohio Yearly Meeting. The greater the confusion or conflict the more clearly we are made mindful of God as the source of a love which is abiding, a love without which we cannot truly love one another.

In counterpoint with these articulating events the steady flow of the meeting continues. Meeting for worship on Sunday morning is our central corporate experience, but in addition many in Cleveland Meeting find that other Spirit-led gatherings, large and small, whether they be earlier on Sunday morning, during the week, or at individually appointed times, are also an important way to grow in the Light. . . .

Quentin Quereau, clerk of Ministry and Oversight Committee

Excerpt from State of Cleveland Meeting, 5/1995
(to Lake Erie Yearly Meeting):

The past year has been a very eventful one for Cleveland Friends Meeting. Eventful times have their own special character which can alternately sharpen or obscure our ability to be attentive to the Inner Guide. We have tried to be attentive. This has led us to focus on spiritual community and how it can be nurtured. We are a very diverse group but trust we have one common agenda—to hear and follow the will of God.

Building community, when folks live many miles from one another and have full and demanding lives outside of the Meeting, is a challenge. We have found that how we handle our relationships within and outside of the Meeting is directly dependent on our relationship with God. Our struggles to identify how God works in the lives of two women in our meeting led us to an understanding that they were acting in accordance with Truth as they were led and with the belief that "Love makes a family." We are reminded of Jesus' answer when told his family was waiting. In

September we celebrated their relationship and family with great joy in a called meeting for worship.

In November, as a result of our witness, Cleveland Meeting was disowned by Salem Quarterly Meeting of Ohio Yearly Meeting. Individually and corporately we experienced sadness, pain, anger, and other emotions and have continued to experience them in changing ways in the months since then. We are trying to find a patient path of love through these conflicting feelings: love for one another and love for members of Salem Quarter and Ohio Yearly Meeting. The greater the confusion and conflict the more clearly we are made mindful of God as the source of a love which is abiding, a love without which we cannot truly love one another.
. . .

From Monthly Meeting minutes, 6/25/1995:
4. We have heard the letter to Ohio YM, which will be printed in the *Tatler*. It is being sent to members of Ohio YM Representative Meeting, members of OYM Ministry and Over-sight Committee, and monthly meeting clerks. David Male remembers that God gave us to understand it was not our business to name the relationship of Nancy Reeves and Lynn Clark a marriage or not a marriage but that it is our business to find a way to express our love to these Friends, and our response was to express it through celebration. The minute from the Committee, 6/3/1993, which took the couple's relationship under the care of the meeting, noted this would "probably require our celebrating and witnessing this relationship in a special called meeting in the manner of Friends."

5. We have prayed for each person present today.

6. We are informed that because of insurance practices, inheritance law, and Emma Reeves's continued access to Lynn Clark if something should happen to Nancy Reeves, it is important for Lynn to legally adopt Emma. It would be helpful if we, as their faith community, send a character reference type of letter to the court in support of the adoption. We approve that Ministry and Oversight Committee draft such a letter, and it be sent over the Clerk's signature.

8. We have heard a letter from Putney, VT Monthly Meeting affirming Cleveland Meeting's willingness to recognize the lesbian relationship between two of our members. They offer their "support and good wishes" to us "for following a difficult spiritual path and to say that it is a path which we believe to be in keeping with the Truth of the Living Spirit." They also sent copies of their open letter of "Welcome to Lesbians and Gay Men" and the "minute of exercise" and explanation of how it came about. We note that the Pendle Hill Pamphlet, *Marriage*, written by one of their members, Leslie Hill, was the source of the quotation of George Fox which was instrumental in facilitating our own understanding of our situation. We ask that a note be sent to Putney Meeting, including a copy of the report (6/3/1993) of the clear-

ness committee as well as this minute. It is suggested it would be useful to discuss in another venue the materials Putney Meeting sent us.

Lois Edgerton, Clerk
Marty Grundy, Recording Clerk for the day

Letter approved by Monthly Meeting, 6/25/1995:
Dear Friends of Ohio Yearly Meeting,

Since Eleventh Month 1994 Cleveland Friends Meeting has existed in a state of separation from Ohio Yearly Meeting. Whether this separation was requested by or forced upon Cleveland Meeting remains ambiguous in the eyes of many Friends, and we feel that it is in the best interest of everyone to state clearly and truthfully what happened.

The facts as we see them are that Cleveland Meeting has not sought, and does not seek, separation from Ohio Yearly Meeting; we have sought and continue to seek to act in accord with God's will. We believe that God is a God of unity and that in following God's will and guidance we are brought into unity and not into separation. If Ohio Yearly Meeting feels it necessary to disown Cleveland Friends Meeting, we ask that this be done clearly, directly, and publicly without ambiguous language which implies that Cleveland Meeting sought or requested the separation. To do otherwise is to fall short of the truth and to evade Quaker process as we understand it.

Cleveland Meeting has followed what we believe to be Quaker process in reaching this point. Starting in 1986, we unsuccessfully approached the issue of same gender marriage in several different ways. The process was painful and spanned eight years of repeated efforts involving a large number of people. Finally, a clearness committee deliberately containing members with widely varying views on the topic was created with the specific charge not of examining the issue of same gender marriage but of determining how Cleveland Friends Meeting should support the family which comprised Lynn Clark, Nancy Reeves, and Emma Reeves.

The committee struggled through many meetings and numerous periods of silent prayer and worship. The committee members felt that they had explored every option available to their human resources and had failed to find a solution. When it appeared that all hope of unity was gone, the committee agreed to pray for one another and fell again into silence, seeking God's guidance. The silence was profoundly deep. Emerging from the silence and looking within their hearts, the committee members were amazed and gratified to find that where there had previously been confusion and disagreement, there was now a clear understanding of God's will in this situation. God had led them to the realization that it was not given to Cleveland Meeting to name the relationship among these family members; it was instead the Meeting's responsibility to celebrate and support these our friends in their joyous commitment to each other.

The minute to this effect from the Clearness Committee was heard in Meeting for Business Sixth Month 27, 1993, but was not approved at that time. The matter was raised again for prayerful consideration at every subsequent Meeting for Business without finding a sense of the meeting to accept it. It was finally adopted by Cleveland Friends Meeting at its Annual Meeting on Fifth Month 22, 1994. The acceptance was not perfunctory; during consideration of the issue at this Annual Meeting, all members present felt God moving within their hearts. This was a powerful experience and there was much joy.

We chose to follow what we believed to be God's will for us, as experienced directly by the members present in Meeting. We did not and do not view this as an act of separation but as an act of submission to divine will according to Quaker process. Therefore, we ask that Ohio Yearly Meeting closely examine its own Quaker process in this matter and that the actions of all of us be clearly recorded.

We feel that these issues must be addressed in order to achieve this end:

- According to the minutes of Salem Quarterly Meeting held Eleventh Month 12, 1994, the "Discipline does not say how a monthly meeting is to be disowned but we recognize that this is what has happened today, even though there is not unity on this course of action."

- Discrepancies exist between this minute of Salem Quarterly Meeting and the same issue as addressed by Representative Meeting of Eleventh Month. The minutes of Representative Meeting record that it considers "Cleveland Meeting released from membership with Ohio Yearly Meeting" rather than disowned. We feel this implies that the separation was at our request.

- The minutes of Representative Meeting also record that a copy of the Representative Meeting minutes documenting the separation of Cleveland Meeting from Ohio Yearly Meeting were to be sent to the clerk of Cleveland Meeting. For whatever reason, we have not yet received this document.

The communion between Cleveland Meeting and Ohio Yearly Meeting over the years has brought much to our monthly meeting, and it is our sincere hope that this has not been a one-way exchange. Some of our members have learned a great deal from Ohio Yearly Meeting ministers and others, and are deeply grateful. Our meeting has been enriched by this association and the process that we have followed in this matter has its roots in Ohio Yearly Meeting. We grieve about this separation. We wish that this process could have happened without causing you pain. Regardless of the formal relationship between Cleveland Friends Meeting and Ohio Yearly Meeting we pray that God's wisdom and love may be with us all.

Signed on behalf of Cleveland Friends Meeting, Lois Edgerton, Clerk

Letter to the court [*missing first page?*]

We, as their faith community, have observed Emma's growth and development. She is a happy well-adjusted child. We have seen that Emma views both Lynn Clark and Nancy Reeves as her parents. She clearly is benefiting from having two parents who love her and have made a commitment to care for her.

In September 1994 Cleveland Friends Meeting took the Reeves/Clark family "under its care". This phrase is the one used when a Friends meeting recognizes and celebrates a union—the meeting takes the union and resultant family "under its care." We realize fully that the State of Ohio does not yet recognize same-gender marriages, but the Society of Friends has a long tradition of recognizing unions and families not yet recognized by the state. The prime example of this in earlier generations was the recognition of interracial marriages when they were not yet legal. In all generations we have recognized and supported unions which we see as mature, responsible, and loving.

The constitution of Emma's family, on a day to day basis, will not change regardless of the court's decision. But granting the adoption guarantees her continuing legal and other rights with respect to both parents, rights most children and parents take for granted (for example, access to medical insurance, inheritance not only from Lynn but from members of Lynn's family, continued access to both parents and/or extended family in the event of Nancy's death). We see this as clearly being in young Emma's best interest.

We believe that in order to protect Emma's rights and to guarantee her access to benefits each of her parents can provide, it is necessary that both of her de facto parents be recognized as her legal parents.

Thank you very much for allowing us to testify on behalf of Emma in favor of her adoption by Lynn Clark.

On behalf of Cleveland Friends Meeting,

Debra Frantz, Clerk

Minute Approved at Friends for Lesbian and Gay Concerns Meeting for Worship with Attention to Business, 7/6/1995

It is fundamental to Friends' faith and practice that we affirm the equality and integrity of all human beings. Equally, we hold that the purpose of recognizing and affirming committed relationships is to strengthen our families and communities.

Therefore, it is our belief that it is consistent with Friends' historical faith and testimonies that we practice a single standard of treatment for all committed relationships.

Given that the State offers legal recognition of opposite-gender marriage and extends significant privileges to couples who legally marry, we believe that a commitment to equality requires that same-gender couples be granted the same rights and privileges.

Therefore, we believe that the State should permit gay and lesbian couples to marry and share fully and equally in the rights and responsibilities of marriage.

We invite Monthly Meetings, Yearly Meetings and Quaker Organizations to consider a minute of support for legal recognition of same-gender marriages, and to communicate this support to their elected representatives.

Because of pending legislation and litigation, we urge a timely response.

From Monthly Meeting minutes, 7/30/1995:

6. Dian Killian is coordinating the organization of the midwinter FLGC [Friends for Gay and Lesbian Concerns] meeting and is sponsoring a planning meeting at our meeting house on 9/9-10. Dian invites the Meeting to join them on Saturday lunch from 12-1 and worship from 1:00 to 2:00. Dian requests the Meeting's help with lunch on Saturday and a brunch on Sunday. The Hospitality Committee will assist. Sue Hogle also offered to help with lunch and Connie Bimber offered to assist with Sunday brunch.

7. The meeting focussed for a few minutes on praying for each other.

8. Lois reported that yesterday was Salem Quarterly Meeting. Ginny Sutton, a member of Stillwater Meeting of OYM, who lives in Philadelphia, felt called to attend and asked Cleveland Friends to attend to hold her and the meeting in prayer. Dian Killian, Marty Grundy, Jody Taslitz and Connie McPeak attended. They reported that Ginny's concern was based on what she had heard and read about our disownment. She was concerned that the issue of homosexuality is a common one among many Friends meetings and other religious communities and suggested that we all need to listen better and pray more for one another. Ginny was also concerned about whether disownment is the best way for OYM to deal with differences, and the Quarterly Meeting's lack of unity when it took the action last Eleventh Month. Martha Giffen, a recorded minister of OYM, also attended. There was no response to Ginny's concerns and hence it was difficult to assess whether she was heard. Martha Giffen called for more honesty about what has happened, stating that Cleveland Meeting may have disassociated itself from Salem Quarter but Salem Quarter has disowned Cleveland Meeting and this needs to be acknowledged. Ginny expressed concern for the health and life of OYM. Ginny felt we should undertake a process of listening to see whether we could hear each other, but that we may not be ready yet. Perhaps it could begin a year from now. Cleveland Friends expressed gratitude for those who attended yesterday's Quarterly Meeting.

Lois Edgerton, Clerk
Debra Frantz, Recording Clerk

*Letters came in from a number of individuals and meetings. Here is an excerpt from one dated 8/**14**/**1995** reporting on North Carolina Yearly Meeting (Conservative)'s annual sessions.*

As far as I know, the subject of Cleveland Meeting's disownment by Salem Q. was not mentioned as an official matter of business but I believe there was some informal incredulity expressed by those who heard of it. The element that would take such action in our yearly meeting is so small that many members are hardly aware of it. Furthermore, the yearly meeting has not yet discussed the matter as a yearly meeting (and our quarters are not very active). This year the matter of same-sex unions was brought up early in the sessions and it was decided not to discuss it this year. Three meetings have accepted minutes that allow for consideration of requests for oversight of same-sex unions. I know we must discuss it sooner or later and that those who oppose such minutes or are uneasy about them must be heard.

C. T.

From Monthly Meeting minutes, 8/27/1995:

7. Marty read a letter from Salem Quarterly Meeting expressing their appreciation for the past sharing between us and their concern that we all wait prayerfully for an opportunity to discern how the Lord would have us proceed. They shared their prayers for us and requested our prayers for them. Friends expressed the concern that others may wish to hear the letter from Salem Quarter and suggested it be read next month.

8. Marty also shared a letter from Kevin Salerno of Palm Beach Meeting expressing his concerns for us in light of our disownment. The letter will be posted.

Marty Grundy, clerk for the day
Debra Frantz, Recording Clerk

Letter from Salem Quarterly Meeting

To members of Cleveland Meeting:

At Fifth Month Quarterly Meeting, the desire was expressed that a message be sent to you, telling of our continued love and concern for you as individuals and as a meeting. We have always valued the contribution that Cleveland Friends made to the Quarterly Meeting and miss this close association.

We all need to discern how the Lord would have us proceed from this point. The hurts and misunderstandings seem to still be too fresh for useful discussions to take place now, but both groups need to be prayerfully waiting for such an opportunity. Ps. 27:14 says "wait [in faith] on the Lord: be of good courage, and He shall strengthen your heart: wait, I say, on the Lord." This is a process which can not be hurried.

Please know that we love you and we pray for you, as we hope you pray for us. Let us all let the Holy Spirit guide us to the truth.

In His love, Salem Quarterly Meeting

Letter from Kevin Salerno, Palm Beach Monthly Meeting, Florida, 7/31/1995

Greetings and peace dear Friends,

I send to thy Meeting my love, warmth and concern. Thy "disownment" is felt by myself and many in my Meeting for the pain, hurt, and harshness that it is. We do hold thee in the Light for God's hand to give comfort and help in healing from the "silent violence" that was laid upon thee. And we have much love for thee.

I have spoken from the Silence to ask my Meeting to hold thee in the Light, we have published in our newsletter our concern to send our written thoughts and warmth to thee, such concern was also sent to *Friends Journal* for publishing in the "Forum" column, and yesterday I presented before my Meeting the history and cause of this issue. I do hope that many send thee their love. Be strong, and have much faith and reason guide thee in knowing that thou does bring forth the continued revelation of our Lord's Light and Love. In much love,

Kevin Salerno

8/1995 Jody Taslitz, David Male, and Liz Beasley attended Ohio Yearly Meeting's Representative Meeting and the Representative Meeting of Ministry and Oversight. Although there was no mention of Cleveland Meeting in M&O, there were a number of personal conversations, indicating that OYM is not monolithic in its understanding of either the issue of same-sex relationships or condoning the process used at Salem Quarterly Meeting.

From Monthly Meeting minutes, 9/24/1995:

4. Lois read a letter from Martha Giffen calling us to find God within the storm. She shared her grief that the spirit was shut out and Quaker process was ignored at Ohio Yearly Meeting and acknowledged pain that we all experience in this separation. She shared also her confidence that Jesus will be victorious in time.

Lois Edgerton, Clerk
Debra Frantz, Recording Clerk

Letter from Martha Giffen, Stillwater Monthly Meeting of Ohio Yearly Meeting, 8/12/1995

Dear Friends of Cleveland Monthly Meeting,

When the winds begin whirling over the oceans gathering up speed then come crashing onto the shore in full hurricane force, is God in the storm? When the clouds gather moisture and become heavy laden with rain then deluge the earth with a flood, is God in the storm?

When the earth trembles, volcanoes erupt and the rocks are torn asunder in an earthquake, is God in the storm? We are told over and over in the Bible that God is in the storms. God speaks and the storms obey, Matthew 8:27. When we find ourselves surrounded by the storms of life we must search until we find God in the storms. We must never call the storms evil, rather seek to focus our energy and attention on praising the Creator of all things. God allows storms to challenge our faith. We are called to worship and adore God and by so doing we allow God to bring good to ourselves and to others caught up in the storms. We learn to find peace within and throughout the experiences. We experience Jesus speaking to our condition and we are changed.

At Ohio Yearly Meeting the report of Salem Quarter went through business without change or sufficient waiting with the Lord. Many of us felt a deep sense of grief that the Holy Spirit was not allowed to do a full work within and among us. Quaker process, as I know and understand it, was ignored.

Ohio Yearly Meeting has followed a fuller process in other situations. When concern was expressed over the inactivity of Uniontown Monthly Meeting in 1991, Short Creek Quarter was asked by the Yearly Meeting to continue in their efforts and report back in 1992. At that time the names of Uniontown Monthly Meeting members wishing to remain a part of OYM were incorporated with Short Creek Monthly Meeting members. In 1983 John Schofield asked Representative Meeting to lay down Chesterfield Monthly Meeting. They directed him to Stillwater Quarterly Meeting. A committee was formed and the concern was brought to the floor of Ohio Yearly Meeting in 1985. By allowing the concern to continue those in attendance experienced a valuable exercise with the Lord. John Schofield has passed on to his reward in eternity and Chesterfield Monthly Meeting continues to exert an influence in a community that sorely needs a center of peace and healing, a place to come and experience Christ in the living silence.

This year that fuller process did not take place. There was no listening to a pleading for corporate Quaker process. There was insufficient listening to allow a response to a call for definition of disownment of an entire Monthly Meeting. There was no openness for a plan for listening to all sides of the issue of same sex lifestyle and homosexuality. Eight years of wrestling within Salem Quarter over these issues has left deep spiritual scars within many. Those of you in Cleveland Monthly Meeting and in Salem Quarter know this more personally than I.

I still weep when I think of your pain. I weep when I think of the spiritual exercise we of Ohio Yearly Meeting were denied in the push to avoid any further discussion of this issue so painful to many. I weep, yet I know that I cannot touch your pain. Only Jesus can touch your pain and show the way to healing. I weep, yet I have faith unshakable that Jesus will be the victor. Not one of us will be spiritually the same as we work through this pain together and with our Lord. I weep, yet I continue to seek in my heart to forgive, to love, to understand, to learn God's lessons for me and for others. What is to be learned is too vast for me to comprehend, yet I trust the omniscience of God to bring us together as pieces of a puzzle, bit by bit, until the picture is complete and we are, once again and more fully than ever before, united in and by our Lord.

I write this letter as one, deeply desirous to continue a spiritual exercise with you and others similarly concerned. I know there are others in OYM who have not stepped forth and I trust that in time they will trust enough to become a part of further exercise with you. I was most encouraged to learn of your plan to share and invite others to share spiritual journeys. This is a most appropriate start to begin rebuilding your faith and seeking clearness of direction to pursue your understanding of the scriptures, your love and your forgiveness.

In the precious love of our Lord Jesus Christ,

Martha S. Giffen

There were several letters written to individual members of Cleveland Meeting from Friends in OYM disagreeing with what happened at Salem Quarter. They were not "official", nor were they to the meeting. But they do show that OYM was not of one mind on this. There were also a number of verbal comments and stories personally shared with members of Cleveland Meeting. Individuals in Cleveland Meeting who were not happy with the situation sought fellowship in Middleton and Winona Meetings.

Excerpt from a letter from a member of Middletown Monthly Meeting, Chester Quarter, Philadelphia Yearly Meeting, 8/16/1995:

Thank you so much for gathering information about Cleveland Meeting's process for responding to same-gender marriage. It has been and will continue to be a great source of help to us. Middletown has just begun the process and we appreciate the hard work you and your meeting and other meetings have done in searching for the Center. Perhaps after enough meeting communities have done this, Friends will be able to see all sides of the truth of this clearly and we will not need to struggle so much with each other.

In God's peace, A. S.

Excerpt from Letter from Community Friends Meeting, Cincinnati, 9/1995

As you may know, Community Friends Meeting (Cincinnati) recently approved a minute recognizing same-sex marriages and also held a same-sex marriage ceremony under the care of the meeting. We hold dual affiliation with Ohio Valley Yearly Meeting [FGC] and Wilmington Yearly Meeting [FUM]. Our actions were reportedly the topic of much heated discussion at WYM in August with some calling for our disownment. A WYM study committee has been formed "to seek information and guidance in developing the Yearly Meeting's position on this concern."

WYM's Miami Centre Quarterly Meeting (of which we are a member meeting) has scheduled a threshing session on our action at its November meeting.

Not surprisingly, then, I was interested in the Spring '95 FLGC Newsletter account of OYM's disownment of Cleveland meeting because your meeting gave recognition to a lesbian relationship in your meeting. . . .

F. B., Presiding Clerk

Excerpt from the Salem-Upper Springfield Monthly Meeting of Friends Newsletter, Fall, 1995 [postmarked Oct. 17]

Yearly Meeting

It was one of the exceedingly hot and humid weeks which this area of Ohio experienced this past summer. The lofty ceiling and brick walls of the Yearly Meeting House did help to moderate the heat. . . . A number of interesting visitors contributed to a good experience, but Cleveland Friends were missed.

The Disownment of Cleveland Meeting was reported in Friends Journal, Nov. 1995, pp. 28-31.[*]

The Disownment of Cleveland

Cleveland meeting was founded in the 1920s and was independent through much of its history. As an independent monthly meeting, it became involved in the Lake Erie Association, which included western Pennsylvania, parts of West Virginia, eastern and northern Ohio, and part of Michigan. Lake Erie Association was initially under the care of a committee of the American Friends Service Committee. Friends World Committee for Consultation undertook oversight after its formation in 1937. As Lake Erie Yearly Meeting formed in the early 1960s, Cleveland Meeting not only joined LEYM but also applied for membership in Ohio Yearly Meeting (Conservative), one of several yearly meetings in the state of Ohio. Ohio Yearly Meeting accepted Cleveland Meeting into membership in Salem Quarterly Meeting, and by several accounts, the relationship was beneficial to all concerned.

As more fully described in a letter to Friends of Ohio Yearly Meeting, which follows [see above, pages 67-70], in 1986 Cleveland Meeting began to seek God's will for them on same-gender marriage. Several bodies in OYM also considered the topic, and there were exchanges of minutes. In 1993, while still laboring with the general questions of same-sex unions, Cleveland appointed a clearness committee to respond to a letter from a lesbian couple asking, first if the couple were clear in thinking they were married as far as God was concerned, and second, how the meeting might take their relationship and family under its care. The clearness

---

[*] ©1995 Friends Publishing Corporation. Reprinted with permission. To subscribe: www.friendsjournal.org.

committee reported in June 1993: "In four meetings we dealt with the easy issues, then we laid our own hopes and expectations on the table and saw their divergence. We tasted despair that we humans could figure out a way forward." They also, however, reported a break-through experience of unity that led the committee to recommend that the meeting was not to name the relationship a marriage or not a marriage, but was to witness to it.

The following minutes of Salem Quarterly Meeting for Ministry and Oversight were recorded in July 1993:

> Last Fifth Month Cleveland Monthly Meeting for Ministry and Oversight brought our attention to some matters that have deeply distressed us. Although their expressed purpose was to seek our prayers, as we pray we are often given understanding. . . . Letters from Winona, Salem, and Middleton Monthly Meetings for Ministry and Oversight unanimously express those meetings' disunity with any recognition of a same gender marriage. As Friends of Jesus we do not mean to condone sin in ourselves, nor in others. We encourage all to live in righteousness. The Bible as well as our *Discipline* state that marriage is a blessing of the Lord and reserved for a man and a woman. It has been recommended that this cause of discord, which separates Cleveland from the three other monthly meetings, be settled quickly. We hope our disapproval is a loving warning that God's judgments cannot be changed to accommodate our own desires. As fellow members of Salem Quarterly Meeting, what each one does is the responsibility of the whole Quarterly Meeting. Although our spirits have greatly grieved in this consideration we are grateful to Cleveland for sharing this burden with us, because it has caused us to go to our Lord in a deeper way.
>
> We appreciate that a Cleveland committee for clearness is convinced that they have been led of the Lord in their deliberations. We also feel that they should consider the concerns of the other three monthly meetings. We desire that everyone concerned feel our deep love and that hearts not be hardened. We seem to have two different directions of understanding and neither feels that the other is willing to listen or acknowledge as valid their direction. We all must continue to seek God's direction.

And in October 1993 they added:

> It is suggested that if Cleveland Meeting does honor and recognize the couple as married in God's eyes they have chosen not to honor the Bible or our discipline. In this decision they would separate as a meeting from Salem Quarterly Meeting. Jesus does not condemn individuals, but he does call us each to repentance and holiness in our lives. We find no Biblical basis for a marriage between two men or two women. Our Ohio Yearly Meeting discipline is also clear that marriage is between a man and a woman.

Cleveland Meeting united with the report of the clearness committee in May 1994. A special meeting for worship was held September 13, 1994, in which the couple renewed their covenant with one another and the meeting took their relationship and family under its care. In November 1994, Salem Quarterly Meeting minuted:

> With the exception of the representatives from Cleveland Meeting, most but not all Friends present feel that Cleveland Meeting by its action has disassociated itself from Salem Quarterly Meeting and Ohio Yearly Meeting. The Discipline does not say how a monthly meeting is to be disowned, but we recognize that this is what has happened today, even though there is not unity on this course of action. Friends would like Cleveland Meeting to know that it can be reinstated if they change their behavior.

Cleveland's letter to Friends of OYM, which follows [see pp. 65-67], describes their understanding of this process. Cleveland Meeting continues in membership in Lake Erie Yearly Meeting.

Ohio Yearly Meeting met in August, and FRIENDS JOURNAL asked Bill Samuel, a member of Adelphi (Md.) Meeting, Baltimore Yearly Meeting, and an affiliate member of Rockingham (Va.) Meeting, Ohio Yearly Meeting, to report on OYM sessions. His report on page 30 reflects the many, deep-seated, conflicting opinions that remain in OYM.

-Eds.

Ohio Yearly Meeting Sessions
by Bill Samuel

As Ohio Yearly Meeting (Conservative) gathered for its annual sessions in August 1995, action regarding the separation of Cleveland Meeting from the yearly meeting was not on the agenda. Membership of monthly meetings is determined by quarterly meetings in Ohio's polity. In November 1994, Salem Quarter effectively disowned Cleveland from membership in the quarter, and therefore in the yearly meeting. That same month the Representative Meeting of OYM acknowledged that Cleveland had been "released" from OYM.

While the matter of Cleveland's membership in OYM did not require yearly meeting action, it was on the hearts and minds of a number of Friends at the sessions. A considerable amount of time in both the business meetings and in the meetings of the Yearly Meeting of Ministry and Oversight was devoted to the expression of concerns on this matter. Much of the consideration might best be summarized in the form of questions not always raised explicitly, but behind many of the expressions of Friends.

Ohio Yearly Meeting sessions did not answer these questions, but did recognize the pain that lay behind the many expressions of Friends. The Yearly Meeting of Ministry and Oversight expressed in its message to OYM a concern about ministering to the pain in Cleveland Meeting, Salem Quarter, the rest of OYM, and those Friends who had felt led to leave their meetings. This did not lead to a structure for that ministry. Friends expressed concerns that they not act in their own wisdom, but wait for the Lord's leadings to be felt by individuals among them.

Many visitors to OYM feel "something special." What is it? Is it a faithfulness to Jesus Christ as Lord and Savior, and the Scriptures as a guide to how he calls us? Is it an opportunity to feel welcomed into a loving community working not to rush Quaker process but always to be guided by Christ's loving spirit? Is this something special preserved and strengthened by a clear stand against that which the Scriptures condemn? Does the something special include an openness not reflected in a disownment?

Will the strong stand embodied in the separation of Cleveland make OYM more attractive to those looking for a model of faithfulness to Jesus Christ? Will a disownment cause many young people to turn away from the witness of OYM because they feel cut off by such action?

Do we need "a marriage of opposites" to give perspective to the struggle between our will and God's will? Or does history teach that Wilburites must not unite with those with a different perspective on Quakerism, as they will be swallowed up if they do?

Are same-gender relationships something the Bible clearly calls us to condemn? Or is it an issue on which Christians can legitimately differ?

Was Cleveland Meeting truly led by the Holy Spirit in celebrating and supporting the relationship of two women? Or was it another spirit in Cleveland Meeting that brought it to that position?

Did Cleveland abandon the discipline of OYM by taking its action? Should it have waited to take such action until and unless the yearly meeting as a whole was convinced that this was God's will? Should the quarterly and yearly meetings have respected Cleveland's action as its best attempt to be faithful?

Were the eight years in which other OYM Friends labored with Cleveland as it considered this issue enough time to be prepared to take the step of separation? Would love and good order require a continuation of the labors until all were in unity?

Was the meeting at which Salem Quarter came to the point of separation with Cleveland one held clearly under the Lord's guidance? Or was it not rightly ordered, forging ahead when there was not unity?

Does love always require that we not separate from those with whom we have significant differences? Can an action taken in the cause of Truth be that of truly loving Friends even though it breaks certain ties?

FRIENDS JOURNAL *has tried to present a balanced account of recent events in Cleveland Meeting and Ohio Yearly Meeting, but we depend upon our readers to let us know how we've done. The* JOURNAL *seeks to explore a wide variety of concerns that are troubling Friends. The editors invite responses.* [italics in original]

From Monthly Meeting minutes, 2/25/1996:
7. Lois Edgerton read a letter from Wyoming Friends Meeting applauding our "careful and considered deliberations" on the subject of supporting a same gender relationship in our meeting, and sharing our hopes that a wider unity may yet be possible.

Lois Edgerton, Clerk
Debra Haines Frantz, Recording Clerk

From Monthly Meeting minutes, 3/31/1996:
8. Other business:
•Lois read a letter from Northampton Friends Meeting in support of our efforts in the area of same-gender relationships and the associated difficulties with other groups of Friends who do not share our views in this area.
•Liz Beasley raised a concern that in the aftermath of being severed from OYM over same-gender issues, some Friends may see us cast in the role of victim, and we may in fact be at risk of so labeling ourselves. Given that neither we nor OYM have done everything right in this matter, we need to give significant thought to ways of moving forward with love and compassion to ensure that we do not become complacent.

Lois Edgerton, Clerk
Wm. Beasley, Substitute Recording Clerk

Excerpt from Letter from Northampton Meeting (New England YM)
. . . We write . . . to extend our wholehearted support to you as you struggle with your connection to the larger community of Friends, as well as with the issue of same-sex relationships.

We feel that the disownment of your Meeting mirrors the experience of many gay people when they come out to their families. These families sometimes move to sever relations with the one who has come out to them. We recognize the pain inherent in such a decision, because we know so many who have endured it, and we feel that such severing denies that of God in everyone. . . .

We honor your courage in remaining steadfast to your calling in these matters. We support you as you struggle to be faithful to the demands of continuing revelation.

Becky Jones, Clerk of Northampton Meeting

From the *Tatler*, 4/1996:
Pam Heggie and Nancy Newman report that in March the court approved Nancy as Lydia's legal adoptive mother. Seven local friends were witnesses while Lydia's moms answered their lawyer's questions and the lawyer signed the papers. The judge was a substitute for the regular one, and was very amused when Lydia sneezed in the middle of the hearing. That was Lydia's only verbal contribution during the hearing. Very reserved of her, considering the possibilities, her moms report. The judge said he

had read the affidavits from family and friends that morning, that he was impressed with them, and that this adoption was *clearly* in Lydia's best interest. Celebration that evening included Lydia's first taste of rice cereal.

From Monthly Meeting minutes 6/30/1996 [14 people present]:
6. A concern from Conrad: Conrad Lindes shared with the meeting his concern related to the Quaker peace testimony, in the form of a suggested testimony extending the peace testimony into areas related to human sexuality. There was vigorous discussion, and appeared to be agreement that the issues involved are of deep concern to Friends and deserve intense examination with the hope of ultimately clarifying areas of agreement and controversy.

George Streeter volunteered to examine Quaker literature and report back to the meeting with a summary of what has been written to date by Friends concerning these topics. Chris Hall raised the point that the distinction between "consensus" and "sense of the meeting" may become critical in these matters.

The meeting will consider the various ways of approaching these topics, such as worship sharing, and consider it again at an upcoming meeting for business.

Lois Edgerton, Assistant Clerk
Wm. Beasley, Alternate Recording Clerk

State of the Meeting Report for Lake Erie Yearly Meeting, 1996

It seems to me that Cleveland Friends Meeting has been resting from the turbulence surrounding our disownment. An integral part of the resting has been that individuals have been trying to go deeper and to strengthen our connections with God and with one another. This is, I believe, the healing work we need to do.

We have been struggling with issues of disownment within the meeting and perhaps within ourselves. There are several of us who do not feel safe in meeting, Some do not feel heard. Some feel judged as being less than others.

Some of the feeling of being judged seems to lie in how we hear those around us and some lies in our failure to connect spiritually with those around us in the embrace of God's love before we speak. Sometimes we hear only the words that trouble us but do not give God the opportunity to translate the message for us in our hearts. Sometimes we cannot share our ministry without being attached to how others hear it. . . .

Finally, I feel we can best move forward by exploring together how we can help one another "own" our contributions to the meeting—both positive and negative. If we learn to be honest about our gifts and the needs we have that would allow us to better use them, we may also learn how to better understand and nurture each other's gifts. If we can be honest about our struggles and loving to those who most challenge us, we may find we can go deeper as a community and discover some of the unity we seek.

Debra Frantz, incoming clerk

From Monthly Meeting minutes, 7/28/1996:
Lois read last month's query and the proposed response. The meeting approved it with one minor change. (Response printed below.)

10. It was asked if we are sending a representative to Ohio Yearly Meeting. Discussion followed and it was decided it is not appropriate to send representatives. However, visitors can attend, so individuals are encouraged to do so.

11. Last month Conrad Lindes proposed a testimony concerning sexual responsibility. It seems right that before we take it up, the meeting receive a report from the Sexuality Committee named last year, the bibliography of resources being prepared by George Streeter be circulated, and perhaps we learn the tools offered by Debra Frantz on spiritual types.

Lois Edgerton, Assistant Clerk
Respectfully submitted, Thomas Cooke, Recording Clerk

The meeting apparently only addressed the first two parts of the query, reserving the last part for the following month.

Response to the Query (approved 7/28/1996)

<u>What has God taught us? What have we learned? What light does this shed on the challenges we now face?</u>

We acknowledge that we tend to be a group of intellectuals who are finding that intellect does not solve all our problems, nor does intellect by itself bring us closer to God.

We are developing a sense of our corporate identity: not as a therapy group but as a religious community. We cannot supply everything hurting individuals need or think they need or want. But we can support and accompany people on their spiritual journeys. We can pray for and with each other.

We are beginning to learn that we alone cannot "fix" things, nor do we need to. What we need to do is ask God for help and guidance, and then to wait until we sense what is God's will in each specific situation.

When we jump ahead of God it doesn't work well. We are learning how easily pride, or fear, or a desire to control, or any other ego-driven motive can lead us to do things impatiently, not to listen to others who differ. We need to confess that sometimes we have been prideful.

We have had an experience that when we listen deeply God can bring us into unity. When we realize we cannot control the situation, that there is nothing we can do, and we wait patiently on the Lord, we have found ourselves in true unity in God's presence. There has been real joy. This hasn't happened often, but it *has* happened.

We are learning that perhaps the most important function of prayer is how it changes the one who prays. Similarly, an ongoing lesson is to experience how communal prayer might change us, corporately.

We are starting to learn that disunity has value. Differences show us we are not yet completely aligned with God, we are not yet where we should be. Recognition of differences needs to be coupled with respect for each other. Community involves a variety of different people (not homogenous clones) who are brought together by God for God's purposes. Community should not be the goal but the by-product of paying attention to God *together*. Disunity should not be side-stepped, feared, or ignored. It is part of the process of learning how to hear and obey God. As we learn to listen past words that divide us, we will probably find more unity than we suspect.

We are learning that enough of us recognize the possibility of change and growth in each other, in the meeting, and in the wider world, that we are learning how to encourage and give space for growth to occur. It is a never-ending task, in spite of discouragement, opposition, or other obstacles. Disunity will always recur; it can be helpful as long as we don't sweep it under the rug. We are learning that people and situations that seem difficult are opportunities for spiritual growth.

We are beginning to learn that God is in charge, not us. We are beginning to glimpse that God offers love, not with outwardly imposed rules but with the Spirit of Christ present within and among us, teaching and guiding, and drawing us toward being that which we are created to be.

From Monthly Meeting minutes, 8/28/1996 [16 people present]:
5. Lois Edgerton reviewed the ways in which we are addressing Conrad Lindes's concerns around the connections between our sexuality and our spirituality with regard to how we behave and how we raise our children. The question remains whether we need to set standards. Liz Beasley will be bringing a report from the Sexuality Committee. George Streeter has prepared a brief background paper and literature review on the issue which is available in the meeting library. Friends are encouraged to read and discuss this information. In addition Debra Frantz will be leading the meeting through some exploration of our spiritual diversity and how understanding and truly embracing this diversity might lead us into greater unity on such critical questions. Friends were asked to consider whether there are other actions that would assist us in considering these issues and in then discerning what God would have us do for ourselves, our children, and the community around us.
Lois Edgerton, Assistant Clerk
Debra Frantz, Acting Recording Clerk

From Monthly Meeting minutes, 9/29/1996:
9. Lois Edgerton presented our response to Eighth Month's query: "What have we been taught by God? What have we learned? What light does this shed on the challenges we now face?" The Meeting accepts this response.

Debra Frantz, Clerk
Thomas Cooke, Recording Clerk

Query Response (approved 9/29/1996)
What have we been taught by God? What have we learned? What light does this shed on the challenges we now face?

We have individually and corporately made mistakes. We have individually and corporately found ourselves getting ahead of God. We have also experienced moments when we knew we were in unity with God and each other. This experience has helped us to understand the importance of waiting for God to lead. When we experience unity we must be sure it continues into the follow through. When we do get ahead of God we need to acknowledge it and ask for guidance on the next step.

We are now experiencing a feeling of being unfinished, of needing to clean house. Homosexuality is still an unresolved issue. How to mend bridges with Ohio YM is an issue. How we show our love is an issue. How we identify, acknowledge and nurture gifts is an issue. How we develop and nurture community is an issue. As we acknowledge gifts, how we deal with our differences becomes an issue. What we teach the children is an issue. Jesus' advice to Martha can help us with each of these issues. The fact that there are various gradations of Christianity offers us a challenge. We grow by learning one step at a time, turning constantly to God. We may not be shown a way to go immediately, but patience and faith in being shown in God's time will bring the unity we seek. One first step we will be taking is going through the book *Discovering Your Spiritual Type* together in an attempt to understand our spiritual differences.

From Monthly Meeting minutes, 11/24/1996:
4. Dian Killian read a recent article in the *Gay People's Chronicle* regarding a woman in the Medina Church of the Brethren who was cast out and banned from the church due to being a lesbian. In this article the Church of the Brethren was compared to Quakers. Tom Cooke read a letter he and Dian wrote and would like to send to the *Gay People's Chronicle* regarding the link between Quakers and Brethren and that Cleveland Friends Meeting is welcoming to gays and lesbians. The meeting approves sending the enclosed letter in the name of the meeting over the signature of the recording clerk. Tom and Dian will investigate whether the *Plain Dealer* printed a similar article, and if there was a similar article Tom and Dian are authorized to send a similar letter.

5. The meeting approves listing our meeting for worship in the *Gay People's Chronicle*.

Debra Frantz, Clerk
Tom Cooke, Recording Clerk

Letter to the Editor of the *Gay People's Chronicle*
To the Editor:
In your Nov. 22 issue you ran an article concerning a woman who was cast out and barred from the Medina Church of the Brethren for being a lesbian and marrying a transsexual. In the article it is stated that the Brethren "are a pacifist congregation similar to the Quakers". The Cleveland Meeting of the Religious Society of Friends (Quakers) would like your readers to know that while Quakers and Brethren share a peace testimony and are pacifist, there are significant differences. An important difference is we recognize the Light of God in all people including lesbians, gays, bi-sexuals, and transsexuals. Our meeting includes several openly gay and lesbian members and two years ago the Meeting recognized the committed relationship of a lesbian couple. We welcome everyone to worship with us on Sundays at 11:00 a.m. at 10916 Magnolia Drive in the University Circle area.

Cleveland Friends Meeting,
Tom Cooke, Recording Clerk

From the *Tatler*:

An important post script: On Tuesday 12/3 the *Gay People's Chronicle* phoned me to authenticate my letter. During our conversation it became clear they did not understand the letter was not from just me, but from the Cleveland Friends Meeting. After describing the Quaker process used to send the letter, the *Chronicle*'s representative said, "I'm quite impressed, and I'll let our readers know this isn't just a letter from you, but from the Meeting."

Tom Cooke

1997

From Monthly Meeting minutes, 1/26/1997:

4. Elizabeth Peacock and Eric Lee requested that they be married in the manner of Friends. After some discussion, it was noted that there is a difference in being married "in the manner of Friends" rather than "under the care of the meeting". Procedure appears to be that a clearness committee be appointed, meet with the couple, and be present at the ceremony. A committee named includes Conrad Lindes, Connie Bimber, Bill Mize, Connie McPeak, and Chris Hall.

Further, it was discussed that Cleveland Friends Meeting's position on same-gender marriages has not been finalized. Friends approved a called meeting to be around the Query: "Shall Cleveland Friends Meeting treat same-gender couples with the same process that we use for heterosexual couples who ask to be married under the care of the meeting?"

Debra Frantz, Clerk
Thomas Cooke, Recording Clerk

Called Meeting for Business, 3/9/1997

1. Third Month, 9th day, 27 Friends met in silence for a called meeting for worship with the purpose of discussing the Query: *Shall Cleveland Friends Meeting treat same gender couples with the same process that we use for heterosexual couples who ask to be married under the care of the meeting?*

2. Clerk Debra Frantz opened the meeting by announcing the purpose of the meeting and having Marty Grundy read selections from past monthly meeting minutes and reports regarding the history of same gender marriage in Cleveland Friends Meeting. Clerk Debra Frantz read selections from the London Yearly Meeting Faith and Practice.

3. After hearing prayerful testimonies and loving witnesses, Cleveland Friends Meeting has found unity that Cleveland Friends Meeting shall treat all couples with the same marriage clearness process that Friends have used for the past 300 years. We explicitly understand that the word couple refers to any heterosexual or homosexual couple who request marriage under the care of the meeting. Further, we hope that through this process we will make ourselves available to God for discerning which marriages should be taken under the care of the meeting.

4. We will hold in prayer until the next meeting our concerns about how we will share the unity we've experienced with the wider community.

5. Meeting for worship with attention to the above mentioned Query ended at 4:20 p.m.

Debra Frantz, Clerk
Tom Cooke, Recording Clerk

From Monthly Meeting minutes, 3/23/1997

5. Clerk Debra Frantz briefly noted that at our "called meeting for business" on 3/9/97, where we reached unity on the process of marrying couples under the care of the meeting, due to the expression of many other issues and concerns we were unable to fully experience the unity we arrived at and to express the joy of this unity. The other issues that were raised will be addressed at meeting for business Fourth month. The clerk invites us now to remember and invite the unity we came into.   Debra Frantz, Clerk
Tom Cooke, Recording Clerk

From Monthly Meeting minutes, 4/27/1997

7. Sharing minute with whom? The minute on same-gender marriage from the recent called Meeting was printed in the March *Tatler*. Friends are urged to read it and pray on it; at a future Meeting for Business (after annual meeting) we will take up the issue of its distribution.

Debra Frantz, Clerk
Wm. Beasley, Temporary Recording Clerk

From Monthly Meeting minutes, 6/29/1997

The Clerk opened the meeting by reading Psalm 121. The subsequent silence was broken by Quentin Quereau, Clerk of Ministry and Oversight Committee, reporting a Judge's refusal of the adoption of a seven-year-old by a member of the meeting. The judge's objection was the gender of the member being the same as the child's mother. The meeting finds the two women proper and fully accepted, and the care of the daughter excellent. The Ministry and Oversight Committee Clerk read a proposed letter to the Judge requesting the reversal of the judge's decision, citing that the adoption of the daughter by the mother's companion is in the child's best interest. With one addition the letter was approved.

During the discussion, there was one objection (qualified as without the intent to interfere with the sending of the letter) to the daughter's conception. This seemed to one Friend to implicate the meeting in condoning something that is not right. The feelings being strongly felt included previous events, which were described as outside the way of the Society of Friends. Here there was expressed an angry statement, about similarity to power plays, the accusation was added that the meeting concentrates on one topic and doesn't progress to other important topics. A concern over enunciating our religious principles seems lacking.

The gathered meeting was recalled where unanimity followed the experience of God's approval of our accepting the established family. The Clerk of Ministry and Oversight Committee made sure the sending of the letter was to proceed as proposed. The member of the meeting's criticisms had included a number of relatively personal feelings; the promise of prayerful discussions along the lines of his topics was offered by the Clerk. The matter of teaching of religious principles was felt important for loving consideration and prayerful thought. . . .

Debra Frantz, Clerk
George Streeter, Recording Clerk for the Day

From the Tatler, Seventh Month 1997

As the meeting further considers C.L.'s concern regarding sexual activity outside marriage, Ministry and Oversight Committee encourages all to prayerfully consider the place of rules and resistance to rules in their lives. This might include consideration of the opposite end of the rules/resistance spectrum from the one you are drawn to. In other words, if you are a person who feels rules are important, consider the places where you resist rules or feel they must be flexibly applied; if you are a person who tends to resist rules, consider the places where you find yourself feeling that there are firm rules which apply. M&O will further consider C.L.'s concern at its August 20th meeting in preparation for bringing it back to meeting for business at a future date. If you have experiences, insights, or leadings which you think might be helpful, please share them with one or more members of Ministry and Oversight Committee.

Quentin Quereau, Clerk of Ministry and Oversight Committee

From Monthly Meeting minutes, 7/27/1997

5. The Clerk read the report from Ministry and Oversight on C.L.'s Concern regarding sexual activity outside of marriage, as it appears in this month's *Tatler*, and suggested that the Meeting prayerfully consider it as a query. Friends reported various concerns regarding rules and the way they should be followed, from and in the Christian tradition, as Friends, and from their own experience. One Friend voiced that the most important rules are written on the heart, but that as a group, it would be helpful to name and recognize what these rules are so that we would all be better able to support each other in observing and following these rules. Other Friends spoke of how the most important "rule" was listening to and following the Light within, that they did not want to be obedient to God's rules as rules but as a result of living in God's Presence. Other Friends spoke about the Peace Testimony, how it holds up an ideal for us to follow, and that other testimonies might be helpful for Friends to agree upon and strive to follow. Another Friend observed that Christ, when pressed, avoided giving many absolute rules and emphasized instead only two: to love God and your neighbor as yourself. Another Friend spoke of how "rules" can vary from culture to culture and that instead of formulating (universal) and absolute rules, it could perhaps be more helpful to seek the Truth. The Clerk observed that further prayerful consideration of this question (regarding rules and how best to follow them) would probably be helpful to the Meeting.

Debra Frantz, Clerk
Dian Killian, Assistant Recording Clerk

From Monthly Meeting minutes, 10/26/1997

4. In recognition of employment discrimination practices surrounding sexual orientation, Dian Killian asked that the meeting send a letter to Congress supporting ENDA, the Employment Non-Discrimination Act. Dian's letter, as approved, is printed following the minutes.

Debra Frantz, Clerk
Kate Spry, Recording Clerk

Letter from the Meeting to our members of Congress
Dear Representative,

The Cleveland Meeting of the Religious Society of Friends (Quakers) urges you to support the passage of ENDA (the Employment Non-Discrimination Act).

Throughout the country, qualified, hardworking Americans are being denied job opportunities, fired, or otherwise discriminated against for reasons that have nothing to do with their performance and abilities. Employment discrimination based on sexual orientation, whether such orientation is real or perceived, effectively denies qualified individuals equality and opportunity in the workplace. Those who experience this form of discrimination have no recourse under current federal law or under the Constitution as it has been interpreted by the courts.

The Employment Non-Discrimination Act (ENDA) would prohibit discrimination on the basis of sexual orientation, providing basic protection to ensure fairness in the workplace for Americans who are currently denied equal protection under the law. ENDA does not create any "special rights" for lesbians or gay men, It simply affords to all Americans basic employment protection from discrimination based on irrational (and unGodly) prejudice.

As Friends, we recognize the Light of God in all people, including lesbians, bisexuals, and gays. Historically and today, many Quaker meetings have witnessed to and acted on behalf of human rights., Employment protection is one of the most basic. As such, we urge you and your fellow Congress members to pass ENDA.

On behalf of Cleveland Friends Meeting,

Jody Taslitz, Assistant Clerk

Nothing more appeared to be done on the topic of same-sex marriage until Ohio seemed poised to pass a bill defining marriage as between one man and one woman.

2003

Minute approved 2/3/2003:

The Cleveland Meeting of the Religious Society of Friends (Quakers) regrets the anticipated action of the State of Ohio to limit the legal benefits and sanction of marriage to couples consisting of a man and a woman. We hold to the truth that it is God who joins two people together in marriage; while a government may hold power to withhold legal benefits and even to deny some couples equal protection, it does not have the authority to marry or deny marriage.

We recognize that there are passages in the Bible that condemn promiscuous and idolatrous homosexual acts; but we find nothing that addresses the question of committed, loving, monogamous same-gender relationships. We have discovered that when we offer unconditional love it becomes easier for us to open ourselves to God's leadings and to have the courage to let go of our personal desires and idols and move into more faithful obedience to God. Our task is to learn how to love the way Jesus loved his disciples and asks us to love one another. We direct each other to the law God has written on each of our hearts.

Members of our Meeting know many same-gender couples that very clearly are married. They have made commitments to love and cherish each other in riches and in poverty, in sickness and in health, till by death they are parted. We see many of these couples raising children with love and wisdom, and we see the fruits of their obedience to God: "love, joy, peace, patience, kindness, generosity, faithfulness, gentleness, and self-control. There is no law against such things." (Gal 5:22 NRSV)

We have seen the blessing of God on their unions, on their families, and through them on the wider community. Our Testimony of Integrity calls on us to witness to what we have seen with our own eyes. It is our hope and our prayer that the State of Ohio will reconsider the ill-named Defense of Marriage Act and recognize the visible truth of these marriages.

William Beasley and Cindy Maxey

2004

Once again political action in Ohio prompted our response:

Minute approved 10/3/2004

We, the members of the Cleveland Meeting of the Religious Society of Friends (Quakers) are deeply saddened by the current attempt to amend the Ohio Constitution to limit the legal benefits and sanction of marriage to couples consisting of a man and a woman. We hold to the truth that it is God who joins two people together in marriage; while a government may hold power to withhold legal benefits and even to deny some couples equal protection, it does not have the authority to marry or deny marriage.

We recognize that there are passages in the Bible that condemn promiscuous and idolatrous homosexual acts; but we find nothing that addresses the question of committed, loving, monogamous same-gender relationships. We have discovered that when we offer unconditional love it becomes easier for us to open ourselves to God's leadings and to have the courage to let go of our personal desires and idols and move into more faithful obedience to God. Our task is to learn how to love the way Jesus loved his disciples and asks us to love one another. We direct each other to the law God has written on each of our hearts.

Members of our Meeting know many same-gender couples that very clearly are married, including members of our own

Meeting. They have made commitments to love and cherish each other in riches and in poverty, in sickness and in health, till by death they are parted. We see many of these couples raising children with love and wisdom, and we see the fruits of their obedience to God: "love, joy, peace, patience, kindness, generosity, faithfulness, gentleness, and self-control. There is no law against such things." (Gal 5:22 NRSV)

We have seen the blessing of God on their unions, on their families, and through them on the wider community. Our Testimony of Integrity calls on us to witness to what we have seen with our own eyes. It is our hope and our prayer that each Ohio voter will recognize the visible truth of these marriages, and vote to reject Issue One.

Nancy Reeves

Four years later, after some former members left and new ones came who had not been part of the preceding deliberations, the issue rose again.

2008

From Monthly Meeting minutes, 9/28/2008

5. Witness in the World Committee has been looking at gay and lesbian marriages and wondering if our meeting's earlier minutes need revisiting.

Joyce Callahan, Clerk
Marty Grundy, Co-Recording Clerk

From Monthly Meeting minutes, 10/26/2008

4. We have heard a report from Witness in the World Committee, that meets on the first Sunday each month after soup. One issue they have been considering is the Homeless Stand Down....

The other issue the Committee is considering is how to support marriage for gay, lesbian, bisexual, and transgendered people. Questions that came up in the Committee include whether both or one member of a couple need to be a Friend, and if the couple wants a legal marriage or a spiritual union. Research indicates that Quakers across the country vary widely in their response to these issues. John Storhm had initially been under the weight of this; now that he has gone the Committee feels that the most recent Cleveland Meeting minute was specifically in response to the then proposed Defense of Marriage Act in Ohio. The clerk helped them see potential ways they could move forward, which they are considering. Friends recollect that a previous minute—which needs to be found—expressed Cleveland Meeting's intent to treat all couples considering marriage under the care of the meeting the same way, regardless of gender of the couple. There was additional good discussion about a number of aspects, but no further decisions have been united on so far.

Joyce Callahan, Clerk
Marty Grundy, Co-Recording Clerk

2009

From Monthly Meeting minutes, 8/30/2009

6. We have heard an oral report from Witness in the World Committee about our witness to the general public on the issue of marriage. This was sparked in response to John Stohrm's challenge to us last year. The Committee showed us its "Proposed Minute on Marriages and Committed Relationships Under the Care of Cleveland Friends Meeting".

We believe that couples, regardless of the gender of either partner, can make the spiritual and social commitment necessary to create and maintain a family. We consider the commitment undertaken in these relationships by both the couple and the Meeting to be that of marriage.

As a Meeting, we welcome applications from any couple wishing to have their relationship be taken under the care of the Meeting, so long as:
- one of the members of the couple are of the Quaker faith and
- the couple chooses to go through our usual method of clearness for marriage and
- that if clearness for marriage is determined, the couple will conduct their marriage in the manner of Friends.

We also believe that the laws of the State of Ohio and of the United States should provide the same legal status for loving commitments between two people, regardless of the gender of the parties in the relationship.

Friends spoke to the difference between marriage "under the care of the meeting" and marriage "in the manner of friends". Friends are uneasy about becoming a "wedding chapel" but are easy to see a clearly worded statement. We appreciate the work on this minute and ask the Committee to continue and bring it back at a later time.

Joyce Callahan, Clerk
Marty Grundy, Co-Recording Clerk

From Monthly Meeting minutes, 9/27/2009

7. We have heard Witness in the World's revised draft minute on marriage under the care of the meeting. Friends questioned the purpose of this minute, beyond that raised by John Stohrm last year for something to post on the web indicating that we are a welcoming community that will consider marriage regardless of the genders of the couple. We are clear that we do not intend to be a "wedding chapel" for any couple who might wander in. Addi-

tional issues that have come up include our willingness to have a marriage only when one or both partners are members—or can one be a regular attender; what do we actually do when we take a marriage under the care of the meeting; and do we need a general statement of welcoming inclusion that is about more than marriage. We ask Ministry and Oversight Committee to consider all three of these issues.

8. We have heard a report from the Library Committee and agree to have printed and bound a single copy of the records relating to Cleveland Meeting's experience with coming to unity on same gender relationships. Friends will then be able to look at it and decide whether or not to print additional copies and/or make it publicly available. Friends agree that Marty Grundy take some of our old minutes and records to the Friends Historical Library at Swarthmore College, Swarthmore, Pennsylvania, which is the official archive for Lake Erie Yearly Meeting.

Joyce Callahan, Clerk
Marty Grundy, Co-Recording Clerk

From Monthly Meeting minutes, 12/13/2009

Minute 6: Cindy Maxey read a draft minute prepared by the Ministry and Oversight Committee on a minute welcoming all seekers, and expressly clarifying that marriage under the care of the meeting will be handled in the same manner for all couples, regardless of the sexual orientation or gender identity of the members of the couple.

Draft Minute:

Cleveland Monthly Meeting of the Religious Society of Friends welcomes all seekers of Truth, regardless of sexual orientation or gender identity.

We understand marriage to be the lifetime commitment of two adults to love, cherish, and support each other. Legal recognition of that commitment is not necessary to make it a sacred and binding commitment.

Marriage under the care of the meeting involves the lifelong commitment of the Meeting to nurture and support the couple. We normally undertake such a sacred commitment only when at least one individual is a member or regular participant in the Meetings, and when we can expect an ongoing relationship with the couple. We follow traditional Quaker discernment practice to determine whether we can, as a meeting, make this commitment. The process is the same irrespective of gender.

We are grateful for the work of the Witness in the World Committee and the Ministry and Oversight Committee on this matter, and will take up consideration of this minute again at our next meeting for worship with attention to business.

Joyce Callahan, Clerk
Nancy Reeves, Co-Recording Clerk

2010

From Monthly Meeting minutes, 1/31/2010

3. The proof copy of the meeting's experience of finding God's will for us around same sex relationships is being passed around so that as many members as possible can read it before next monthly meeting. We need eventually to decide how many copies should be printed (i.e. how widely to distribute), how to deal with personal names, and if there are additions or deletions to be made. Meeting approves sending a .pdf version to active members and attenders; feedback should be sent to Marty Grundy.

9. The revised meeting minute on same sex marriage is tabled until next month because we do not have the newly revised draft that addresses the issues raised last month.

Joyce Callahan, Clerk
Marty Grundy, Co-Recording Clerk

From Monthly Meeting minutes, 2/28/2010

3. We have heard the revised draft minute on marriage, brought to us by Witness in the World Committee. The Committee also explained how it came to propose the minute and the various amendments and revisions it has undergone. With a few more tweaks Friends approve the statement now as the understanding of God's will for our meeting.

> Cleveland Monthly Meeting of the Religious Society of Friends welcomes all seekers of Truth, regardless of sexual orientation or gender. Friends' testimonies to the Truth include simplicity, peace, integrity, community and equality. Out of the ground of these testimonies comes our understanding that marriage is a covenant relationship between the couple and God, to which we are witnesses. It is a lifetime commitment of two adults to love, cherish and support each other. This sacred and binding commitment is not dependent upon legal recognition of the marriage.
>
> Marriage under the care of Meeting involves the continuing commitment of the Meeting to nurture and support the couple. We normally undertake such a sacred commitment only when at least one individual is a member or regular participant in the Meeting, and when we can expect an ongoing relationship with the couple. We follow traditional Quaker discernment practice to determine whether we can, as a Meeting, make this commitment. The process is the same regardless of the gender of either or both parties.

4. We note that most Friends have not had an opportunity to finish reading the manuscript about our meeting's experience with finding God's will in regard to same sex marriage. We agree to meet Friday evening, April 2, at 7:00 to discuss it.

Joyce Callahan, Clerk
Marty Grundy, Co-Recording Clerk

From Monthly Meeting minutes, 3/28/2010
4. We have heard a letter from Charles Kelly and William Kohler describing their upcoming marriage on Fourth Month 24 under the care of Birmingham Meeting [LEYM], asking our permission to proceed with their plans. We are not aware of any encumbrances or impediments on Chuck, and we trust Birmingham's clearness process. Therefore we ask the Clerk to write to Birmingham Meeting to this effect, and also to write to Chuck and Bill inviting them to come and visit us, and share their joy with us.

9. There are some questions we need to consider in regard to printing something about Cleveland Friends Meeting's experience coming to a sense of the meeting as to what we have been called to do at this time about same sex marriage. The questions are both stylistic and substantive. In the former category are such things as how to more clearly differentiate among types of documents and comments; inclusion of additional material; and font size. Substantive issues include how widely available this should be made, and what to do about the use of names. There will be a meeting this coming Friday, Fourth Month 2, at the meeting house at 7:00 p.m. to discuss these things and any others that may come up on this general topic.

Joyce Callahan, Clerk
Marty Grundy, Co-Recording Clerk

The sense of the meeting held April 2, 2010, is summarized in the Preface. See page 5.

From Monthly Meeting minutes, 4/25/2010
8. An update on the project of publishing the experience of Cleveland Friends Meeting with same-sex relations informs us that additional minutes, letters, and records have been found and keyed in, although there are still a few gaps. The cover has been redesigned slightly. A new preface and introduction have been written. A number of Friends have expressed interest in reading the next draft when it is ready. Those who are interested are asked to give their names to Marty Grundy.

Joyce Callahan, Clerk
Marty Grundy, Co-Recording Clerk

From Monthly Meeting minutes, 7/18/2010
Report of Library Committee
   A report was heard from Marty Grundy about the draft manuscript of *The Experience of Cleveland Friends Meeting with Seeking God's Will in Same-Sex Relations*. It is attached. There were no major suggestions on changes from Friends. The Meeting approves the revised cover and text as circulated and publication with CreateSpace.com.
   Book design decisions will be made by the committee working on book. We leave the discretion of asking for back-jacket com-

ments to the author. . . . If comments are requested, the Clerk or the Clerk of the Library Committee will write letters asking for comments.

In terms of pricing, we need to decide how much marketing will be done and how many review copies need to be printed. An ad hoc marketing committee of Laura Lockledge, Joyce Callahan, Connie Green, and Jo Steigerwald will meet with Marty to discuss marketing the book. The group will then return to Meeting with their recommendation.

Minute of Support

With joy-filled hearts, Cleveland Friends Meeting offers a minute of support for the project that has resulted in the manuscript: *The Experience of Cleveland Friends Meeting with Seeking God's Will in Same-Sex Relations*. We participated in the process of creating this book as a Meeting. It chronicles our attempt to follow God, serving as an example of one Meeting's experience in following a right decision and through it, the deepening of our spiritual practice. We share this concrete history to elucidate who we are and what we are trying to do. Our hearts are filled with gratitude to Marty Grundy, for her years of meticulous record keeping, faithful work, and diligent compiling of documents that comprise this manuscript.

Chris Farrand, Clerk
Jo Steigerwald, Recording Clerk

This minute is printed as the epigraph on page 3.

The editor and committee met and decided to rearrange the title so that it reads: <u>Seeking God's Will in Same-Sex Relations: The Experience of Cleveland Friends Meeting</u>.

From Monthly Meeting minutes, 9/19/2010
Book Update

We have received a proof copy of *Seeking God's Will in Same-Sex Relations: The Experience of Cleveland Friends Meeting*. It will undergo a final proofreading and any changes will be made. This will be followed by another proof copy, and then it will be ready for sale. The book will be available at the Meetinghouse and through [CreateSpace.com and] Amazon.com for $6.50.

Chris Farrand, Clerk
Jo Steigerwald, Recording Clerk

Made in the USA
Charleston, SC
05 November 2010